BUDDHA

A BEGINNER'S GUIDE

GILLIAN STOKES

Hodder & Stoughton

A MEMBER OF THE HODDER HEADLINE GROUP

Acknowledgments

The author acknowledges the help and support of James Pollicott, who also provided the original ideas for the illustrations.

Orders: please contact Bookpoint Ltd, 78 Milton Park, Abingdon, Oxon OX14 4TD. Telephone: (44) 01235 400400, Fax: (44) 01235 400500. Lines are open from 9.00–6.00, Monday to Saturday, with a 24-hour message answering service. Email address: orders@bookpoint.co.uk

British Library Cataloguing in Publication Data
A catalogue record for this title is available from The British Library

ISBN 0 340 78042 8

First published 2000
Impression number   10 9 8 7 6 5 4 3 2
Year   2005 2004 2003 2002 2001 2000

Cartoons by Richard Chapman.
Typeset by Transet Limited, Coventry, England.
Printed in Great Britain for Hodder & Stoughton Educational, a division of Hodder Headline plc, 338 Euston Road, London NW1 3BH by Cox & Wyman, Reading, Berks

CONTENTS

Contents

Right Belief

Right Knowledge

Right Conduct

Introduction

WHO WAS THE BUDDHA?

The **Buddha** was a man named Siddhartha Gautama who lived in northern India nearly 2,500 years ago. He is famous as the spiritual inspiration and founder of the religious path known today as **Buddhism**. Buddha is actually a title and not a proper name. It means someone who is **awakened** or **enlightened** to the nature of life and its meaning. Buddha is a title given in recognition of this supreme spiritual attainment.

The Buddha lived from approximately 563–483 BC (scholars dispute all dates connected with his life and teaching). He is said to have been born on the full moon day of May in Terai, northern India, in the foothills of the Himalayan mountains, near to what we now call Nepal. He led a privileged life from birth, but felt drawn to learn of spiritual truths after realizing the suffering that accompanies life. He therefore left his beloved young wife and new son, his wealth and prestige, to follow the established tradition of **asceticism** or renunciation.

Siddhartha was not given the title of Buddha until the age of 35 when, after six years of spiritual practices, he became enlightened to the truth behind all appearances. From the time of his enlightenment Siddhartha Gautama, the Buddha, also became known as Sakyamuni, the sage or wise teacher of the Sakya people from whom he came, though he preferred the term Tathagata, meaning 'Truthsayer'. Siddhartha saw how suffering is caused by ignorance and desire, and how ignorance can be removed. After his enlightenment he no longer clung to existence or the idea that he had any eternal essence or identity. The Buddha began to

KEYWORDS

Buddha: title given to one who has gained direct knowledge of the true nature of all things. From *Budh*, meaning 'to know, to be awake, to be conscious of'.

Buddhism: the tradition of thought and practice expounded by the Buddha.

Awakened/enlightened: a state of heightened perception and realization of the truth.

Asceticism: the practice of severe self-denial and discipline for spiritual or religious reasons.

teach out of compassion for the suffering of those not yet enlightened to the truth of all things. He travelled widely for 45 years, teaching others how to reach the same understanding and insight. He died of a digestive complaint at the age of 80. His last words are recorded in many reference works as: 'All created things are perishable; work diligently on your own salvation.'

WHY IS THE BUDDHA'S TEACHING IMPORTANT?

The Buddha showed, by personal example, that an individual is capable of reaching such spiritual heights that the mind can open, and can know and understand the truth of all reality. He was living proof that this can be achieved without reliance on faith or divine intervention.

The Buddha taught in the spoken dialect of the people, rather than in the formal Sanskrit language of traditional religious texts. This made his teaching accessible to an audience who could not read, and who up until then had relied on priests to interpret religious thought. The Buddha did not set out to conflict with

KEYWORD

Sangha: a Buddhist community of monks, and nuns supported by the community among whom they live.

people of other religious beliefs. He encouraged reliance on personal endeavour and experience, and the value of membership of a community (the **sangha**) rather than in the scholarly examination of scriptures, external teachers (including himself) or divinities.

HISTORY AND LEGEND

The historical facts concerning the human life of Siddhartha Gautama have become interwoven with many legends, most of which were attributed after his lifetime. These legends drew upon an Indian oral tradition which existed long before Siddhartha's birth. Stories were used to convey religious understanding, ethics and social duties. Over time such traditional tales embellished the recorded facts of the actual birth, life and death of the historical figure of the Buddha, so it is now difficult to extract fact from fiction. The authenticity of what we are told are the words of the Buddha cannot now be verified, though the basic teaching is common to all subsequent Buddhist traditions.

There is little to corroborate events in the life of the Buddha in the surviving Buddhist texts. As far as we know little of his biography was recorded in them, and political upheavals in the centuries since his death have caused many to be lost. We do know that the Buddha Gautama was a real person who extended human understanding by his own effort, and encouraged others to do likewise.

HOW DO WE KNOW ABOUT THE BUDDHA'S LIFE?

Religious stories would be learned, told and retold by storytellers, priests or monks who travelled from village to village. Tales such as the *Mahabharata* and the *Ramayana* – vast collections of Hindu and Brahmanic legends and epic material – were later remembered and communicated to people in this same way, most of whom had no access to other forms of mass communication. The telling of these tales was a mixture of theatre and religion. The listeners learned theology, ethics and the duties expected of them through the example of the fabulous characters and divine beings who populate the stories.

THE BUDDHIST ORAL TRADITION

Some who heard the Buddha speak decided to practice what he taught. Following the established Indian tradition these religious seekers left their homes, possessions and all former attachments, took the Buddhist vows and entered the sangha (community). The sangha provided the monks with support and a disciplined routine without harsh austerities.

The monks who formed these early Buddhist communities also took to reciting the words of the Buddha rather than writing them down, since this was tradition, and writing materials were scarce. These memorized teachings eventually became known as the *Pali Canon*. In this way the Buddha's teaching was learned word for word while he was still alive, according to

> **KEYWORD**
>
> *Pali Canon:* a collection of Buddhist teachings written in Pali, the spoken language in which the text had been learned and transmitted orally.

the recollections of those who had heard him speak. These memorized teachings were regularly recited by the monks in the sangha. This served to preserve the teaching in the time-honoured way, and to share it with those who had not heard the Buddha directly. However, the emphasis was on the teaching, not the factual life of the Buddha.

BIOGRAPHICAL DETAILS

Little was memorized about the events of the Buddha's life beyond the major events, as far as we know. This is not surprising as we are told the Buddha always deflected attention from himself to the teaching. No written material is directly attributable to the Buddha and none was written even close to his lifetime. This does not mean his teaching was unreliable however.

Efforts were made soon after the Buddha's death to ensure the various oral recollections were consolidated. As the Buddha had lectured for about 45 years without recording anything, this was a huge task. To this end, a council of all the communities was convened (the first of many). This took place during the year after the death of the Buddha (between 485 and 542 BC), and lasted for several months. The aim was to affirm what had been memorized, and to agree on a unified version. The recitations were approved, though not without some dissent. This council also set out the future rules for all monastic life.

A century after the Buddha's passing (or so we believe) a second council was convened at Vaisali, today known as Basarh in Bihar state, to re-evaluate the accuracy of the oral transmission at that time, and to contain a rebellion from some monks who wanted to relax certain aspects of monastic discipline. Efforts at con-

KEYWORD

Mahayana: school of Buddhism that introduced mystical elements and the possibility of complete nirvana for all.

tainment were not successful and the rebels parted from the main order. They subsequently rejected some of the rules concerning monastic discipline and reinterpreted others to redefine the Buddha as a supernatural being, a revelation said to have been mystically inspired by the Buddha himself. These changes led to the formation of the **Mahayana** school of Buddhism.

The oral transmissions continued for several centuries until, with the spread of Christianity and Islam, there came a drastic reduction in the number of monks and nuns available to memorize and maintain them. This threatened the very survival of the teaching, so it was decided to write down all of the *Pali Canon* for the first time. This was almost six hundred years after the Buddha's death. It was also after disagreements and modifications had affected some of the recollected material. When the *Pali Canon* was written, a third section on philosophy was added. Councils have been held ever since whenever it is thought the records need to be purified or major decisions made.

THE LOSS OF RECORDS AND TEXTUAL RELIABILITY

There is another reason why we have little direct access to the life of the Buddha today. Not all of these texts, written centuries after he lived from oral source material, have survived. Wars and political interventions have led to the loss and destruction of many of them. Some had been transcribed and translated into other languages as Buddhism spread, notably into Chinese. Also the number of texts has expanded as commentaries were added and different communities recorded their recollections. These translations represented a massive task, added to which the concepts used in one language did not always translate accurately into another. The textual information about the life of the Buddha that we have has been pieced together from scattered references in the texts that survived this difficult passage, from later commentators and from reference sources beyond the Buddhist community.

Although the memorized words of the Buddha were written many centuries after he spoke them, and texts were subjected to many tribulations, we have no reason to believe that the factual material contained in them has been altered. The discipline surrounding the learning and reciting of sacred material was traditionally strict, and the recollections were revered. So, despite all that has happened, some of the surviving texts may well recall the actual words spoken by the Buddha. Some will be the recollections of those who knew him and heard him speak, and some will be a record of the teaching as it had developed by the time it was recorded. Our problem is, we have no way of distinguishing which is which. We have no scriptural testament directly attributable to the Buddha, and no authorized written version of the events of his life, nor of his direct teaching. What we have is a record of the living practice of his teaching as it has passed from monk to monk, and nun to nun, and as it has adapted in the light of understanding and circumstances. However, this would seem to be what the Buddha wished for it.

❊ ❊ ❊ ❊SUMMARY ❊ ❊ ❊ ❊

• The Buddha was a real man called Siddhartha Gautama who lived in northern India approximately 2,500 years ago.

• Siddhartha discovered all creatures experience suffering, though he had been protected from this by his father. He left his life of wealth and prestige and his loving family to find liberation from this inevitable fate.

• For six years Siddhartha struggled to control his body and free his mind, suffering austerities of all kinds before he realized this was not the way any more than was his life of riches.

• A middle way between these extremes and long meditations brought the Buddha to a state of enlightenment seated beneath a Bo tree. He went on to teach what he had learned for the next 45 years.

India at the time of the Buddha

2

INDIA'S RELIGIOUS HERITAGE

The Indian subcontinent has been influenced by the many foreign peoples who have roamed it over the centuries for trade and invaded it for political ends. With these newcomers arrived new religious ideas from the Far East, Greece, the Caucasus region and beyond. Religious seekers were also frequent travellers through northern India in ancient times.

Hinduism

Hinduism is the largest religion in South Asia today, and is one of the oldest continuous religions in the world, despite having no single founder or moment of origin. Like a mighty river created from the many tributaries that fed into it, Hinduism is an amalgamation of the beliefs of the many people who settled in India in ancient times. For this reason Hindus have no single holy scripture and have worshipped different deities at different periods in history. The word *Hindu* is a corruption of the Persian name for a river we now call the Indus. Hindu merely designates a person who lives in the land beyond the Indus river, and refers as much to the culture as to its diverse religious beliefs. To be Hindu is thus to live a religious life in accordance with sacred law and the duties expected of society.

Modern Hinduism is defined by the presence of certain common religious beliefs. The most important of these is that an enduring essence, or **atman**, transmigrates from life to life, inhabiting many bodies. The nature of one's next rebirth is thought to be determined by the accumulated effects of one's actions in the

KEYWORD

Atman: in the Hindu interpretation this means essential self. Divine breath which permeates man (Aryan early Vedic interpretation).

present and past lives known as **karma**. Karma is considered to be a natural law. Different Hindu sects and cults have different expectations of the end of the soul's journey, but all Hindus share a belief in rebirth according to past deeds. Hindus believe **transmigration** may be into the body of an animal, human, or even of a spirit or minor god in a different dimension. These concepts originated in the complicated development of India's religious history.

The Indus Valley civilization

The earliest form of Hinduism that has been traced was that of the Indus Valley civilization.

KEYWORDS

Karma: cosmic law. The accumulated effect of a person's actions whether for good or ill. The force which causes rebirth.

Transmigration: Continuity of a soul or atman (Hindu), or the process itself (Buddhism). From one life to the next.

Ascetic practices: religious attainment through discipline.

It flourished in the area we know today as Pakistan between 2000 and 3000 BC. Archaeological remains suggest the society rivalled that of ancient Egypt. Though few traces of their beliefs survive, from artifacts it seems the society was egalitarian. **Ascetic practices** and ritual cleansing were important. A mother goddess, and a male deity surrounded by animals have been found on fragments of pottery and other artifacts. (The Hindu god Shiva, surrounded with animals in one of his many aspects, may have been a later development of this deity.) The Pipal tree seems to have been venerated here, a practice still common in later Hinduism and Buddhism. The Indus Valley civilization disappeared at around the same time Aryan nomads invaded from the northeast. Whether the well-established Indus civilization died out because of Aryan intervention or an unrelated natural cause, we do not know.

The Aryan invaders

The Aryan newcomers gradually spread further into India, settling and introducing new cultural influences as they did so. Hinduism from this point is a series of adaptations and resistance to the Aryan influence on local religious beliefs and cultural practices. Later Hindus believed the soul might one day merge with a higher spiritual force or god. Some believed we are already a part of such a divinity and our work is to realize this. Others believed spirit and matter are, and remain, separate and different. The multiplicity of these beliefs reflects the Hindu adaptation to the many religions of travellers and invaders with which it came into contact.

The Aryans came from the Caucasus region, between the Black Sea and the Caspian Sea around the middle of the second millennium BC. They were nomadic herdsmen who brought with them their culture, language and religious beliefs.

Principal among the Aryan rules was **varna**, a hierarchical division of society into different classes of ritual purity. We know this today as the **caste** system (**Jati** in India). This idea was completely at odds with the egalitarian principles of the former Indus Valley civilization. Aryans used **soma** (intoxicants) to achieve altered states of consciousness during ritual ceremonies and sacrifices. Sacrificial offerings were essential in many religious contexts yet the necessary rituals could only be undertaken by a priest of the highest class. This made the other castes dependent on priests for their spiritual welfare.

The focus of worship fluctuated according to prevailing influences. The old belief in female deities was suppressed for a time because the main Aryan deities were male, but later they resumed an important role in Hindu worship. The early Aryan settlers introduced a belief in **Brahman**, a mysterious impersonal force or spirit that permeated the whole universe. Supreme and absolute, Brahman was thought to be ultimate reality, indivisible from the world through which it manifested in countless forms. Such a belief is known as **monism**. According to the **Veda** the inexpressible

KEYWORDS

Varna: original Aryan classes: Brahmana or Brahmins; Ksatriyas; Vaycias; Shudras. The structure of the varna was supposed to have divine origins.

Caste (Jati): social status, class or racial division inherited at birth.

Soma: intoxicant used to induce altered states of consciousness for religious purposes.

Brahman: the Absolute; supreme spiritual force; impersonal, gender-free, and beyond limitations and descriptions. Present in all things.

Monism: the belief in one and only one substance of which all apparent things are merely a part.

Veda: ancient Sanskrit word meaning sacred knowledge. Name given to the collected hymns and texts sacred to the Aryan people.

mystery of Brahman operated no less in every human being than in all the universe.

This early concept of Brahman was of a neutral force, and should not be confused with the masculine creator-god, Brahma, of the much later trinity of Hindu gods. Later Vedic belief incorporated a personal aspect of Brahman, a 'chip off the old block' called *atman* which was also limitless and indefinable. (Note: This early form of atman was the breath of the universal divine through its manifestations, and *not* what we might speak of in later times as the Hindu soul, or self.)

Writing was unknown in these ancient times, so Aryan priests memorized the hymns they composed for use during ritual sacrifices. They passed these on to succeeding generations in an oral tradition for centuries. When the technology of writing eventually developed the hymns were collected together and written down, together with texts describing the magic and sacrificial formulas, and rules for practicing religious services. Most scholars believe that the *Veda* dates back to the thirteenth century BC, and parts are even older. The language used in the texts and in religious ceremonial was ancient Sanskrit, which was familiar only to the religious class.

The Aryans continued to advance further into India. Their influx was not meekly accepted by all the local people however. Fierce battles raged for many years and formed the inspiration for legendary epic literature such as the *Ramayana* and the *Mahabharata*, still beloved by Hindus today.

Indo-Aryan beliefs

Local beliefs adapted and merged with the new Aryan religion over time. By about 600–400 BC there were believed to be 33 Indo-Aryan gods, with Indra as the most important. The gods were thought to be separate manifestations of the one divine being, so worshipping any one of them was a channel or focus to the one, ultimate divine. These divinities were not an abstract concept like Brahman. Divinities could be loved, worshipped and entreated. A creator-god (Indra) was believed to have sacrificed himself, causing the cosmos to be formed from the divine sacrificial remains. According to **Brahmins** it was sacrifice that had created the world and sacrifice was required to sustain it. Since only the elite caste of Brahmin priests was permitted to make sacrifices, the power and influence this gave them in society was profound. (All Hindu priests were Brahmins but not all Brahmins were priests.)

KEYWORDS

Brahmins: the highest caste. Only Brahmins were considered ritually pure enough to become priests.

Upanishads (Vedanta): sacred texts that completed the *Veda* but undermined its earlier teaching.

Religious adaptation was an open-ended process. Intermarriage affec-ted beliefs so the Brahmins abandoned animal sacrifice in favour of non-sentient offerings, for example, flowers or rice milk, but some sacrifice remained essential. The Hindu cult beliefs were taken over by these Brahmin priests who in all respects acted as intermediaries, both for the gods, and for those who sought their blessings. Deities were believed to have a direct and personal influence on human life, so by performing sacrifices or good works, divine reward and good karma were thought to follow.

Upanishads
Ascetics had always existed alongside the formal religions. They claimed to attain spiritual truths without the intervention of priests, sacrifices or rituals. This appealed to a people who were becoming disillusioned with the priests' wealth, power and exclusive claims to divine access. Asceticism gave individual seekers a hope of escape from the wheel of rebirth.

As asceticism gained in popularity, texts describing ascetic practices and philosophy, called the *Upanishads* (or the *Vedanta*), were added to the *Veda*. This was around the time that the Buddha lived, or soon after. The addition of these mystical and speculative texts to the *Veda* completed it, bringing together the two main streams of religious endeavour, the priestly and the personal. Its inclusion captured the mood of the time but undermined the authority of the earlier texts and threatened the religious exclusivity of the priestly caste, the Brahmins.

The personalization of divine contact introduced in the esoteric teaching of the *Upanishads* necessitated changes in beliefs about Atman, which was now seen as the highest potential within humankind. Atman now became personalized as a self or soul that transmigrates from one body to another after death. This version of Atman offered individuals the potential to merge with Brahman, like drops of water returning to the sea, or sparks to the flame. At the time of the early *Veda* the divine was believed to be in all, and all was one. By the time of the *Upanishads* it was speculated whether we are many, but all have within us a spark of the divine. Later still, Hindus would wonder if the spark within is actually identical with Brahman, the divine, and it is our idea of individuality which is the illusion.

According to the ancient law of karma, the effects of past actions accumulate and disperse throughout many lifetimes and this belief was also now incorporated with the belief in a personal Atman. The quality of one's next birth would be determined by the nature of one's karma. According to the *Upanishads*, to realize the indivisibility of the inner Atman and Brahman releases one from the eternal round of rebirth and suffering, and nullifies the effects of past karma.

The Buddha and India's religious heritage

The Buddha lived at a time when old religious practices were falling from favour. He accepted some ancient Hindu beliefs, sought to change some he believed to be mistaken, but above all he encouraged personal verification of what he taught, rather than blind adherence to politically inspired religious practices. A great deal of the Buddha's popularity stemmed from his use of common, everyday language in his sermons, which made his teaching accessible to everyone regardless of class. Much of his teaching opposed Aryan religious beliefs and rituals. He forbade the use of intoxicants, asserted there are no gods, and taught an attitude of non-violent respect for all sentient life, which meant the end of live sacrifices. The communities he organized were a return to egalitarianism such as we believe existed in the Indus Valley before the Aryans arrived. He is said to have intuitively experienced the truth of the law of karma at the time of his enlightenment. The Buddha shared the belief that realizing truth brings liberation, though he differed on what constituted truth. He denied the existence of an eternal soul, essence, or Atman, and the possibility of merging with a higher being or essence.

CASTE AND SOCIAL STATUS

Since the invasion of the Aryan peoples, South Asian society has been ordered according to what we now call the caste (jati) system of ritual purity. The caste system probably originated with the Indus Valley civilization in some form but was later adopted by the Aryans who already had a system known as Varna. The many Indian castes were added to that structure and eventually all south Asian religions accepted caste divisions, though it is now mainly associated with the Hindu religion.

The caste system determines what an individual may and may not do. Social position, employment opportunities, religious obligations, and even marriage partners are determined by one's ritual purity or caste. Caste membership is automatically the right of a child born to parents who are both of the same caste. Distinctions between one caste and another are so great that in practice they are like different nationalities or races. Members of a caste enjoy benefits too. The special skills and knowledge required for the particular work applicable to a caste are jealously guarded by its members. In this way they function somewhat like medieval guilds.

Within each of the principal castes are hundreds of sub-castes today, and the numbers expand as the nature of work changes in modern India to accommodate the new work patterns occasioned by technological change. The practitioners of these new skills are allocated to new or existing castes and their children will then be defined as being of the same caste.

The three hereditary Aryan classes, or Varnas, were:

* **Brahmins:** the priests. Priests are still Brahmins today;
* **Kshatriyas:** royalty, nobility and warriors. The Buddha's family were Kshatriyas, as they were of noble if not royal birth;
* **Vaisyas:** the hereditary Varna of farmers, merchants and workers.

The fourth Varna, the Shudras, was comprised of non-Aryans whose work, not their birth defined their class. They attended to the needs of the three hereditary Varna and so were in close contact with them.

After the Varna, countless modern castes developed, each defined by their inherited ritual purity and the work they do.

The outcasts or untouchables

Lower than the lowest point in the hierarchy were the so-called **untouchables** or **outcasts**. These individuals, as their name suggests, were without caste. Some would have been born untouchable, for example the child of a mixed-caste union, or of a marriage with a foreigner without caste. It was also possible to lose one's

> **KEYWORD**
>
> Untouchable or outcasts: those whose occupation or birth denies them a place within the caste system. The lowest status in society.

caste status through contamination, such as by doing work considered only fit for untouchables. Outcasts announced their presence by ringing a bell, beating a small drum, or by calling out, to give other caste members a chance to avoid touching them (which could precipitate the loss of their own caste status by contamination). Some untouchables performed work deemed to contaminate others to such a degree that they contaminated merely with their presence, even if no contact was made. Some untouchables would therefore only move about at night, when there was less likelihood of meeting or contaminating others. Outcasts were given the work that no one else would want to do, often dangerous as well as unpleasant. They prepared corpses for funerals, or lived by scavenging for items of value from rubbish tips, for example, and had to live outside the village boundary. In the twentieth century, Gandhi, an Indian religious and political leader, compassionately called outcasts the Harijan, which means the children of God. He worked to better their lot and change public perception of them.

The belief in karma helped to make the inequalities experienced because of caste acceptable. One's place in life was seen as the result of one's own past actions. Whether one was a king or lowly born was fair in the long-term. Acceptance of the inevitability of one's lot in life as a result of the caste system and religious beliefs has greatly influenced south Asian culture as a whole. Attempts made to outlaw the caste system, especially in relation to untouchables, as in the 1949 Indian Constitution and since, have largely failed. In cities however the modernization of ideas and lifestyles has lessened or changed the influences gained or lost by caste membership.

THE HOUSEHOLDER AND DHARMA

The three highest divisions of Aryan society were collectively called Varna, or the 'twice born'. This refers to the 'rebirth' of males after initiation, followed by a period studying the *Veda* under the tutelage of a Brahmin. Thereafter these men would maintain the household sacrificial fires and perform minor rituals, under close supervision. Their inherited pure class status made them worthy of these tasks, once trained.

A Brahmin priest would usually have a wife and family and a home to support so he would perform sacrifices every day in his own fireplace, as well as any he might perform in his priestly role for the wider community. Everything in the world was considered to have

KEYWORD

Dharma: natural   law according   to   Buddhism. The teachings of Buddhism.

its proper place, form and function, and the household was no exception. This is **dharma**. In addition to being a word used to describe religious law, dharma can refer to the social traditions associated with ordinary village life, the rules governing correct behaviour and status and in particular the householder's role. The traditional roles and functions, aspects of nature, such as the rain or sunshine, were also dharma, no less than the proper behaviour of individuals, and religious rules.

Buddhism encouraged the renunciation of all these rules in favour of the ethics of personal responsibility. To become a member of the Buddhist community required complete separation from the social world because its demands were perceived as a barrier to achieving detachment.

THE TRADITION OF WANDERING ASCETICS

Religion has been indivisible from everyday life in India throughout history, and religious practice has long influenced social behaviour. Brahmanism predominated, but was not the only faith by the time of Siddhartha's birth. There was an enduring and widespread interest in religious belief and personal spiritual development, especially in the northeastern region of India where he was born. The tradition of renunciation and asceticism was widespread. Traces seem to exist as far back as the Indus Valley civilization. These ascetic seekers would leave their homes and families, renounce all former comforts and allegiances, and wander the countryside. They lived rough, relying on begging to survive. Meditation and contemplation techniques were used to still the mind and encourage altered states of consciousness which, it was thought, would bring one to a deeper sense of understanding. These activities were supported by a traditional philosophy which justified these methods.

Asceticism demanded self-denial, mental training and mortifications of the body, in the belief that a weakened body could be subjugated to the will of the mind. Some wandered naked in all weathers, some imitated the life of an animal, and many undertook prolonged fasts. Many sages and wise men drew interested audiences and attracted disciples from these 'gone forth' as the wandering ascetics were called. Some ascetics chose to become solitary recluses.

The **Jains** were an important sect of ascetics whose ancestry apparently dates back to the

KEYWORD

Jains: ancient Indian religion. Members avoid harming any life form, some even at the cost of their own.

Indus Valley civilization. The Jains were con-
temporaries of the Buddha and are still part of
Indian religious life. Jains take personal
responsibility for not harming any living
thing, a principle known as **ahimsa**. This
necessitated the rejection of sacrificial rituals
such as Aryan, Brahmanic and Hindu philoso-

KEYWORD

Ahimsa: the principle of
non-violence or injury to
living things. Practised by
Jains and adopted by the
Buddha.

phy demanded. The Jains also believed in karma – that all actions eventually produce reactions, and these reactions ultimately have personal
consequences from which the soul may be liberated. Liberation may be
won by an ethical life of truthful interactions, including non-attachment, honesty and chastity. Ahimsa was taken to extremes by some
Jains. Harm to another creature would be paid for in the perpetrator's
suffering, or a bad rebirth. For this reason and from compassion, Jains
adopted a policy of non-action as far as possible. A careless in-breath
might injure a gnat passing by, a step might kill an ant, and even vegetarian food might accidentally cause harm to creatures when harvested
or eaten, so some Jains wore no clothes, some wore a face mask and fil-
tered their water, others even refused all food until they achieved a
meritorious death.

By the time of the Buddha's birth it was far from unusual for a mature
man of good breeding to give up family life and enter on a personal
spiritual quest. Siddhartha himself had been taught by a Jain ascetic
during his spiritual wandering and much of his eventual teaching is
similar to Jain philosophy, apart from the notion of an eternal soul.

✳ ✳ ✳ ✳SUMMARY ✳ ✳ ✳ ✳

- Forms of Hinduism pre-date Christianity by 2–3000 years.

- The oldest known religion in India was that of the Indus Valley civilization.

- Aryan invaders settled in India and introduced many changes into the religious and social lives of the people among whom they settled. *Vedas* were a collection of their sacred texts and Varnas were the class divisions of their society. Aryans used rituals and sacrifices and believed in a divine order, and an enduring essence.

- Asceticism promised the individual escape from suffering without need for a costly priest.

- The *Upanishads* are a collection of texts which describe ascetic philosophy. They spelt the end of the *Vedas* to which they were added.

- The Buddha encouraged personal religious effort and experience regardless of class. He denied the existence of an essence or lasting identity.

Buddha's Early Life

3

THE *JATAKA TALES*

Scholars believe many **Jataka Tales** existed before the Buddha was born. Some can be found in the ancient scriptures of other religions, and even in Aesop's fables, familiar in the West. To Buddhists, however, the *Jataka Tales* relate the exploits of the Buddha in this and his countless previous births (when he was a **Bodhisattva**). The *Jataka Tales* affirm Siddhartha's right to Buddhahood, and set examples for ethical and meritorious behaviour. Difficult concepts such as rebirth and karma, are made more comprehensible by the use of imagery.

These much-loved moral stories serve to emphasize the future Buddha's ethical and

positive qualities, and tell of how he stored up karmic merit. One tale tells of a previous life when he offered his own flesh to ransom a hunted pigeon; another of how, when he was a king, he gave away all of his possessions. Dramatic touches from other well-known ancient legends embellish the stories. Many paranormal events were said to have occurred at key points in the Buddha's life, and these are incorporated in the *Jataka Tales*. Awe-struck and devoted followers have often made such paranormal claims for their religious leaders. Otherwise normal phenomena, such as heavy rain, an earthquake, or a clap of thunder can seem to acquire spiritual importance, and are subject to reinterpretation if they coincide with a great event in the life of a religious person. Whether or not they really occurred, and if so, whether they had paranormal origins, is a matter for personal belief.

Nowhere in the *Pali Canon* is the life of the Buddha recounted in its entirety. No factual biography was recorded until the Sanskrit document, the *Buddhacarita* (*The Acts of the Buddha*) was written by Ashvagohosha, an Indian poet in the first century AD. This was centuries after the Buddha had lived and died, and only separate fragments taken from copies translated into different languages have survived for scholarly examination. These scraps reveal that legend and fact are indivisible throughout stories of the life of the Buddha. The legends are of doubtful authenticity, but are included here because they are common to all stories about his life and are revered by Buddhists. However, the historical facts of the Buddha's life story, which follows, are italicized to separate them from what are probably legends.

THE BIRTH OF SIDDHARTHA GAUTAMA
The conception and birth of Siddhartha, the Bodhisattva, or Buddha to be, were particularly steeped in supernatural legends.

Conception and pregnancy
It is said that Siddhartha's mother (Mahamaya, or Maya) conceived the child 'without defilement' which suggests a virgin birth. She is said to have had a dream at the time of Siddhartha's conception. She dreamed that a Bodhisattva entered her womb in the form of a white king elephant with a red head. This creature descended from the Tushita heaven (traditionally home of contented gods and Buddhas-to-be) and entered her body without causing pain. This was an auspicious sign. The pregnancy proceeded with no physical problems though Maya found herself longing to meditate. She and the king set off for the forest at Lumbini where she could meditate in peace.

The birth
Legends suggest it was an unusual birth. The baby was born from his mother's side, without causing her hurt or pain, ten months after his conception. The birth occurred at the time of the full moon in May, while Mahamaya stood in a grove of trees in Lumbini park. At the moment of his birth it is said a great light covered the earth causing the blind to see, the lame to walk, and prisoners to be freed from their chains. Legends add that all the characters who

would become important in the future life of the Buddha-to-be were also born in the same moment.

The child was said to have been born with the full self-awareness appropriate to one entering his last life. He is said to have walked seven steps and looked to the four corners of the world as soon as he was born, and to have stated: 'For enlightenment I was born, for the good of all that lives. This is the last time that I have been born into this world of becoming.' Torrential rain washed the mother and child following the birth. Mahamaya is said to have died a week later, her work in this life done. Her baby was raised by Mahamaya's younger sister, Siddhartha's aunt Mahapajapati, and his father.

SIDDHARTHA'S FAMILY BACKGROUND
Siddhartha Gautama is known to have been born in Terai on the foothills of the Himalayan mountains in northern India, near to the present-day country of Nepal. His parents were of the Sakya people, members of the Kshatriyas class, and if not royalty, were certainly important local figures. Siddhartha was the son of the local Rajah king, Suddhodana, and his wife Mahamaya, and so was born into a family who enjoyed relative wealth and privilege.

The king, Siddhartha's father, is said to have asked a wise fortune-teller called Asita, what the future might hold for his son. *This was common practice at the naming of a child, in a ceremony traditionally held at the time of the full moon.* The soothsayer was immediately struck with awe at the sight of the baby. He noticed 32 signs on the child's body which prophesied an auspicious life. The soothsayer advised the king that his son might become a powerful ruler, perhaps the Emperor of all India if he became wise in the ways of the world. However, if he were to follow a religious life, these same signs indicated the child could as easily become a great sage, and if he renounced his noble birthright, maybe even saviour of the world. The fortune-teller was desolate that he would not live long enough to benefit from the full grown wisdom of this auspicious child.

A COMFORTABLE LIFE

The child had been given the family name Gautama, after an ancestor who was a famous teacher, and he was now also given a first name, Siddhartha (meaning 'he who has reached his goal'), in expectation of the potential envisaged for him. The king preferred his son to inherit the power and wealth of an emperor rather than become a sage so he determined that the child should know nothing of the life and suffering of ordinary people. Siddhartha was to be prepared for his grand future with a life of comfort and ease. Siddhartha Gautama was raised in this luxurious style by an aunt, his mother's sister Mahapajapati, and his father following the death of his mother. Mahapajapati may have been another of the wives of Suddhodana as polygamy was not uncommon.

FROM CHILDHOOD TO MATURITY

Siddhartha was given several palaces in which to live, according to the season, so he should not suffer intense heat, nor the rains and cold, and in each one every aspect of his life was refined and luxurious. His father saw to it that Siddhartha should know only fine foods and clothes, and provided him with all the sensory delights by which he hoped his son would become ensnared in a life of privilege and reject any thoughts of a religious life. Siddhartha was taught sports, arts, mathematics and other skills appropriate to his class, and he learned them very quickly. He lived a life of ease in the upper storeys of these palaces, away from all the sights and sounds of the common people beneath.

At the age of seven, Siddhartha is said to have attended the annual ploughing festival with his father, the king, who traditionally ploughed the first furrow. He sat at the foot of a rose-apple tree to watch the ceremony and saw how hard the men and animals worked in the sun, and how the ploughed earth damaged plants, and injured or killed small creatures. He watched a lizard catch and eat an ant only to be eaten itself by a snake, which in its turn was snatched up by a vulture. He pondered on this chain of events, and feeling compassion for the suffering he had witnessed, he spontaneously entered a deep meditative state.

MARRIAGE AND FAMILY

In accordance with the normal customs of his people, Siddhartha was married at the young age of 16. It is said he won a series of contests for the right to marry his beautiful cousin Yasodhara who was selected for him by his father. She was said to be desired by many noble suitors but Siddhartha's greater skill at mathematics, sports and the martial arts outperformed all other contestants. In particular Siddhartha drew a mighty archery bow which had belonged to an ancestor and loosed an arrow when rivals could not even lift the bow.

The couple were duly married. Siddhartha and his young wife lived happily in the palaces built for him by his father for many years well apart from the cares of the wider world. Yasodhara gave birth to a son, Rahula (meaning 'chain'), when Siddhartha was 29 years of age.

✳ ✳ ✳ ✳ SUMMARY ✳ ✳ ✳ ✳

• The *Jataka Tales* ('birth stories') relate the exploits of the Buddha in previous births.

• Siddhartha's mother dreamed that a Bodhisattva (Buddha-to-be) entered her womb as a white king elephant with a red head.

• Siddhartha's mother died soon after he was born. He was raised by his father and an aunt.

• Siddhartha's father raised him to be free from worldly cares because he wanted his son to become a powerful ruler and not a spiritual leader, both of which had been prophesied.

• Siddhartha learned about suffering and meditation while watching a ploughing festival.

• Siddhartha won the hand of his bride in a contest when he alone could draw and fire an arrow from a mighty bow.

4 The Search for Truth

LEAVING HOME

Siddhartha was intelligent as well as an able athlete, and he began to wonder about the outside world of which his servants spoke. He arranged for his groom, Channa, to accompany him on forbidden journeys beyond the palace. Despite his father's efforts to keep such sights from him, on each of four such trips Siddhartha discovered examples of the human suffering from which he had been so long protected.

On their first outing he chanced to see an old man. Channa explained how age affects everyone. Siddhartha was shocked and returned to the palace to consider this fact.

On their second excursion, Siddhartha chanced to see a sick man. Again he was shocked to learn that everyone becomes sick sometimes. Once more he returned to the palace, troubled.

On their third journey from the palace, the pair saw a corpse being taken for cremation. This sight and Channa's explanation astounded Siddhartha. How could all these people be going about their lives seeking pleasurable pursuits ignoring the risks of disease, with the certainties of old age and death awaiting them? Siddhartha realized these people were no different from himself, his wife and his child. In that realization he lost all desire for gain, and pride at achievement. He realized that disease, age and death await all, whether insect or king, and now looked with a new compassion on all his fellow beings. He realized with a shock that suffering is an inescapable part of life and lost interest in the sensory pleasures he had formerly enjoyed. They seemed a waste of the little time he had left to understand these dreadful certainties.

Siddhartha and Channa made one more trip together and this time Siddhartha saw a religious ascetic. This man seemed content despite his rags and plentiful reasons for suffering. Siddhartha wanted to learn the holy man's secret, but knew he would never discover it while living his own pampered existence. He was willing to suffer personally if he could also learn to be indifferent to it.

Siddhartha determined to assume his birthright, though not the one selected for him by his father. He would spend the rest of his life in search of answers to these mysteries. He could no longer take pleasure in his former sensual delights, not even in the birth of his son or the love he had for his wife, now he knew these things were impermanent and must end. Siddhartha decided his life must now include uncertainty, impermanence and pain, as well as the possibility of pleasure. He left his beloved family and life of luxury on the same day his son was born to become a humble wanderer and seeker of the truth.

SIDDHARTHA BEGINS HIS SEARCH FOR TRUTH

Siddhartha took his horse, Kanthaka, and accompanied for the last time by his groom, Channa, he secretly left the palace and his old life. Legends say the god Hrideva silenced his horse's hooves on the cobbles so no alarm would be raised. When they reached the river, Siddhartha left all his fine clothes and jewels with Channa, marking the end of his former status and riches. He told his faithful servant to return them to his father with news of his plan to search for salvation or die in the attempt. His father was not to grieve, since in time they would have been parted by death anyway, and not knowing how much time he might have left to live there was no time to waste, the search must begin immediately. Channa was upset to leave his master and tried to dissuade him without success. Sorrowfully he did as he was told. Alone now, Siddhartha cut his princely hair and crossed the river (both symbolically auspicious acts) to become an ascetic wanderer.

KEYWORDS

Mortification: the practice of self-denial or discipline to bring the body into subjection.

Yoga: practical techniques for attaining altered states of consciousness and ultimately liberation from karma and future rebirths.

It is said that Siddhartha sought out teachers who could advise him in the techniques considered necessary for spiritual progress. He dutifully performed the **mortifications** they suggested. He is said to have led this life, of extreme contrast to his former lux-ury, for the next six years.

LIFE IN THE FOREST

Siddhartha now lived in the forest and sought enlightenment according to traditional ways. He practiced **yoga** and listened to the teachings of other ascetics and Brahmin holy men. He was joined by five other seekers who had also renounced their home lives. They were proud of their yogic powers and the control they had over their senses but were impressed by Siddhartha's even greater commitment and the extreme mortifications he suffered in his attempt to subdue his body and liberate his mind. These six seekers lived together beside a river, relying on the generosity of alms and practicing their austerities.

AUSTERITIES AND THE MIDDLE WAY

Siddhartha continued with extreme austerities in this way, gaining in psychic powers but at the cost of his health and physical being. He continued to practice yogic exercises and fasted, eating just enough to keep himself alive until after six years he was reduced to skin and bone. Near death from fasting he realized that although he had gained certain skills, he was no nearer to finding the answers he sought. He realized liberation would not be won by following extreme austerities any more than it would by living his former life of luxury. A more moderate middle way must be the answer.

Siddhartha remained steadfast in his endeavour, but made an intel-ligent re-appraisal of how to achieve his goal. He realized that a body that craves food and drink is too distracted to be able to med-itate properly, and a dead body tells no tales, so he decided to eat just enough to healthily sustain his meditations. He went to bathe in the river but collapsed on the bank, exhausted from the effort. It is said that a young herdswoman saw him there and was moved by the pitiful sight. She offered him some rice-milk which she had been taking to a shrine as a religious offering. Siddhartha gratefully accepted and broke his fast.

Siddhartha now began eating regularly to restore his body to health. His former companions were horrified to see the man whose determination they had so admired now apparently made soft and indulgent again. They criticized Siddhartha for forsaking his quest and abandoned him.

Siddhartha decided to meditate until he reached understanding, or die in the attempt. Recalling how as a child he had accidentally entered a deep state of meditation when seated under a tree to watch a ploughing match, he now made himself a grassy seat under a tree where he remained for days and nights determined to resist the temptations of his mind until he found the illumination he sought.

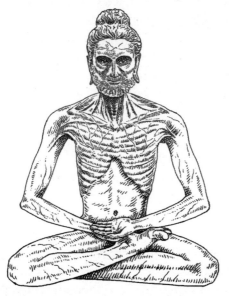

The emaciated Siddhartha meditates.

When it seemed Siddhartha's goal was within reach, Mara, the god of the underworld, brought an army of demons to tempt and distract him, afraid that if Siddhartha attained enlightenment they would lose dominion over him. Despite their distractions Siddhartha remained steadfast in his meditation, and with his right hand pointed to the earth he summoned the earth goddess as witness that his enlightenment was imminent and the forces of evil were defeated.

ENLIGHTENMENT

Siddhartha meditated throughout that night. He remembered his previous births, recalling what he did during them and what his names had been. He saw the lives of previous Buddhas and of those yet to come. (There have been a series of Buddhas, each appearing when the teaching of the last has been forgotten.) He saw how all created things are dependent on previous causes, even our own birth and the seeds of future rebirth are sown by the karma created in previous births. Freed from senses, emotions and desires he now saw with compassion how birth, age, disease and death lead to rebirth on the great wheel of life, because we have this false belief in separate and everlasting identities. He realized it is ignorance of this fact which binds us to **samsara**.

> **KEYWORDS**
>
> **Samsara:** (wandering) the wheel of becoming, of continual life and death.
>
> **Naga:** Half-human/half-divine mythical serpent. Regarded as a symbol of the Buddha's enlightenment.

Surrendering to the implications of his realizations, Siddhartha became liberated from all desire and ignorance which would have caused his own rebirth. He realized everything is impermanent, and everything in the universe changes and decays. At dawn Siddhartha entered into non-conscious ecstasy from which he emerged as a Buddha. Legends speak of the signs by which nature revealed its pleasure: the earth is said to have swayed like a drunken woman, and there were thunderclaps, pleasant breezes and holy rain which mixed with flowers and fruits all falling from the sky. Life rejoiced with the emergence of a new Buddha.

The Buddha continued to meditate under the Bodhi tree for another week after the moment of liberation, and remained in the area for a further seven weeks during which he meditated and performed yogic exercises. During this time, the Buddha's meditation was threatened by inclement weather. The spirit of the lake by which he sat recognized the Buddha for what he had become. This **Naga,** in the form of a huge king cobra snake, wrapped its mighty coils around the Buddha to give him warmth, and shielded his head from the rain by extending its hood over him like a canopy. The Naga's generosity gained it merit towards a better rebirth.

The Buddha protected by the Naga.

✳ ✳ ✳ ✳ SUMMARY ✳ ✳ ✳ ✳

- Siddhartha escaped from his palace and learned of age, sickness, death and religious contentment.

- Unwilling to await inevitable suffering and sorrow, Siddhartha set out to discover a remedy.

- After six years of arduous spiritual practices, Siddhartha realized neither comfort nor austerity could lead to the truth. He decided to try a middle way.

- Siddhartha attained enlightenment after prolonged meditation.

The Teaching Begins

5

THE DECISION TO TEACH

It was common practice in ancient India to devote time to a spiritual quest of one kind or another. There would have been many interested to hear a teacher who claimed to have found truth. However, the Buddha, or **Tathagata**, as he preferred to call himself after enlightenment,

hesitated to teach. For one thing, he knew from his own attempts to learn from other teachers, truth cannot be taught. If truth is to be more than just another memorized intellectual fact, it must be experienced. In addition, the Buddha doubted anyone would willingly accept that all they considered valuable was false. He suspected his listeners would prefer to keep their illusions if the truth threatened their habitual way of life but he felt compassion for the needless suffering their ignorance caused. For some weeks the Buddha continued to meditate at the place where he had become enlightened. Eventually he decided he would at least try to teach those he knew would be interested.

THE FIRST SERMON: THE TURNING OF THE WHEEL OF DHARMA

First the Buddha sought out his five former ascetic companions in the belief they might be able to comprehend what he had learned. He found them at the Deer Park at Sarnath near Varanasi in Benares, northern India. He knew these friends hungered for the truth, so he shared with them what he had realized at the time of his enlightenment and in so doing he set in motion what became called the Wheel of the Law.

The Middle Way

The Buddha explained to his audience that mortifications and austerities are not the way to achieve liberation and enlightenment, any more than a life of sensual indulgence is. He advocated a moderate, middle way which requires vigilance but avoids extremes. This method or path to personal liberation involves commitment and individual effort, but will bring an end to suffering. Regular meditation is essential. No amount of intellectual understanding can replace a moment's insight gained during meditation. His first sermon formed the core of the teaching he would repeat for the remainder of his life. Gautama Buddha did not create the truth he taught – it had always been so – but the teaching of the previous Buddha, Kassapa Buddha was no longer remembered or effective. Each Buddha who revives the teaching is said to turn the wheel anew, but dharma – the truth – is eternal.

The Four Noble Truths

* Suffering is experienced by all living creatures.

* Suffering is always caused by desires for sense-pleasures, to cling to life or as a death-wish.

* Suffering can be overcome.

* Following the **Eightfold Path** (see page 33) will bring freedom from desires, ending suffering in this life, and rebirth.

KEYWORDS

Eightfold Path: the fourth of Buddha's Noble Truths, and the means he proposed to achieve liberation from suffering.

Lay: non-ordained Buddhists who serve the needs of the members of the sangha and thereby gain merit.

Vihara: the building that houses the sangha.

THE SANGHA IS FORMED

The Buddha knew it would be difficult to keep to the Eightfold Path and maintain family life, so he formed an egalitarian community, the sangha, initially of monks, later of nuns too. Living in a community the initiates would support one another and see that the refuge of the teaching, the dharma, was passed on to generations of seekers. Sangha refers to the order of monks and **lay** members. Where the monks lived was called a **vihara** or monastery. The first monks were ordained by the Buddha but as the order grew, existing monks accepted the new members.

The Eightfold Path

The Buddha explained the details of the Fourth Noble Truth which became called the Eightfold Path. If well followed, it leads to liberation and the end of suffering.

1 The wisdom of true understanding
of the dharma
of the law of karma
of the direct experience of emptiness, of no-self
of the Four Noble Truths
of the Eightfold Path
of the traditions of the sangha

2 The wisdom of true intentions and thoughts
of unselfish and generous renunciation, not greed or desires
of love and goodwill to all beings, not ill will or anger
of kindness and compassion towards all beings, not cruelty

3 The morality of true speech
truthful and kind communication of all kinds
the wise use of silence

4 The morality of true conduct
thoughtfulness and consideration in all actions
no killing or harming of sentient beings
no taking what is not given or intended
no cheating
no sensually reprehensible thoughts or behaviour

5 The morality of a true livelihood
useful work which does not harm other beings or the environment
no trading in armaments, slaves, meat, intoxicants or poisons

6 The mental discipline of true effort
develop meditation, insight, intuition and willpower
use effort to avoid wrong thinking
use effort to dispose of wrong thoughts if they occur
use effort to develop right thinking
use effort to enhance and maintain right thinking when it happens

7 The mental discipline of true mindfulness
awareness of your thoughts, actions and feelings
develop the mental states that will bring progress on the path
know your physical body, inner states and surroundings at all times

8 The mental discipline of true concentration
learn to still the mind
observe the capriciousness of thoughts and moods
know all action starts with a thought and learn to think wisely
in stillness learn to see things as they really are

New members all made a declaration, known as the **Three Jewels of Buddhism** (or Triple Gems), declared by all Buddhists to this day.

KEYWORD

Three Jewels of Buddhism (Triple Gems): the Buddha, the dharma and the sangha.

* I take refuge in the Buddha (as proof that liberation ends suffering).

* I take refuge in the dharma (for knowledge and understanding of cosmic law).

* I take refuge in the sangha (for practical and spiritual support).

The Buddha made no firm rules for the sangha at first. He merely asked that its members promise to try to live an ethical life. He had regularly argued with Brahmins over rules and rituals which had lost all meaning and relevance. Monks simply promised that they would:

* not harm any living thing;

* not take anything not freely given;

* forsake the pursuit of sensual pleasures and be celibate;

* speak and think truthfully, kindly and compassionately;

* avoid all intoxicants.

These apparently simple promises are difficult to keep. They apply to all Buddhists, though the laity were not required to be chaste, merely to avoid adultery. Later, more definite rules and practices were introduced in the communities, to maintain discipline and a sense of unity.

The following five promises were additionally required of ordained monks or nuns:

* avoid eating solid foods after midday;

* avoid frivolous entertainments;

* avoid perfumes, body adornments and jewellery;

* avoid using high or luxurious beds;

* avoid handling money and valuables and all monetary dealings.

Detailed accounts of the rules of the sangha survive in the **Vinaya Pitaka** text covering all aspects of monastic existence, especially relations with other members of the community and the lay population whom monks and nuns met when collecting donations of their daily food.

Buddhist ethics were, and are, strict. Any thoughts, speech or actions that harm others will cause harm to the perpetrator, according to the law of karma, so monks and nuns are usually vegetarian. To eat meat contributes to the death of another being. Even to drink milk causes harm, since young animals are taken away from their mothers and killed or abandoned so milk is available for humans. The monks slept on simple beds to avoid too much or too little comfort and possessions were limited to essentials. To possess anything in excess of need is to steal from another who may need it more. Such ethical precepts are challenging and would be harder to sustain outside a community. The path to liberation is for everyone, but few are those who can tread it.

After the Buddha died, when the teaching was being recollected, for what would eventually be the *Pali Canon*, the rules (the *Vinaya Pitaka*) were thought so important they took precedence over the Buddha's own sermons. Compassionate ethics can dictate that rules must be broken in some situations, if greater harm will be done by compliance. The Buddha reminded his listeners what he taught was not intellectualized teachings but truths, which they might also come to realize since truth did not require the presence of a Buddha. As he said in his last sermon, each person must be their own teacher.

THE SECOND DISCOURSE: *SUTTA PITAKA*

This second discourse was given by the Buddha soon after he had ordained a group of former fire-worshippers. He explained to them how they were deceived when they believed that senses are the property of an identifiable self. Using the language they would understand he helped them understand each sense is on fire, with craving, likes, dislikes, attractions and revulsions and this causes feelings and, thereby, misery. The Buddha advised these former ascetics to stop their mortification of the senses, a practice he had shared before he found the middle way. Once freed from such attachments, he said, they might liberate themselves from karma and rebirth. To realize the truth of impermanence and non-self the Buddha asked the following of these former ascetics.

'Is the body we have permanent or impermanent?' To which the new monks replied, 'It is impermanent.'

'And what of feelings, ideas or mental formations, perceptions and consciousness itself, are they permanent or impermanent?' After reflecting a moment, they replied, 'Impermanent, Lord.'

The Buddha now asked of them, 'And are impermanent things experienced as pleasant or painful?' To which they replied, 'They are painful, Lord Buddha.'

Now the Buddha asked, 'Of these things which you have said are impermanent, transitory and painful; which might be said to belong to you and of which could you rightly say, "I am that"?' The disciples responded, 'None of these, Lord Buddha.'

'Then understand and remember', said the Buddha, 'that whatever feelings, perceptions, mental formations or consciousness, and whatever corporality, be it yours or another's, large or small, present, past or future, high or low, far or near, gross or subtle; none of these is yours. These do not belong to you. You are not these, and this is the true wisdom.'

45 YEARS SPREADING THE DHARMA

The Buddha travelled far and wide over the next 45 years, teaching the dharma repeatedly. He ordained new monks and nuns from among any suitable seekers, and formed many new sanghas to perpetuate the teaching. The Buddha rarely chose to answer **metaphysical** questions, saying that there is enough to learn to truly comprehend our situation and live a moral life, without trying to grasp the unknowable. Speculation on what one might experience after death when all sense organs have perished is not a fruitful area for contemplation. The Buddha likened the

KEYWORDS

Metaphysical: The character of existence and reality.

Ineffable: too great for words.

human condition to having been shot with a poisoned arrow. Surely removal of the arrow and treatment for its poison should demand your full attention, rather than waste precious time in wondering who shot it, what wood the arrow was made from, where it was made and what type of bow was used to fire it. We should concentrate on attaining our liberation and not worry what might or might not exist elsewhere. However, the Buddha did take issue with Brahmanic beliefs and state there are no gods or **ineffable** spirits such as Brahman, and no human counterpart or everlasting essence, such as Atman.

The Buddha is reputed to have held listeners spellbound with his lectures and to have convinced them by his wisdom and example. He did not perform tricks or miracles to gain a following as did many spiritual teachers of the time. It was the simple compassion and wisdom of his words that impressed his listeners. He used stories or questions to convey the points he wanted to make. For example, it is said a grieving mother brought her dead child to the Buddha and begged him to restore her to life. Rather than refuse outright or retreat behind intellectual arguments, the Buddha gently asked the mother to bring him mustard seed from a house untouched by death. Perhaps thinking that this was an ingredient for the ceremony that would restore her child, the mother dutifully obeyed. She returned later, made wiser by the impossibility of this task. In discovering death touches every household, rich and poor, she accepted more easily her loss and appreciated the compassionate way the Buddha had consoled her.

✻✻✻✻SUMMARY ✻✻✻✻

● The Buddha doubted that he could teach what he had learned, but compassionately felt he must try.

● The first sermon given by the Buddha is called the 'Turning of the Wheel'. The dharma is said to have begun from that moment.

● The Four Noble Truths state that all living creatures suffer as a result of desires but can be freed by following the Eightfold Path.

● The Eightfold Path states the practices to be adhered to, to attain enlightenment.

● The Three Jewels (Refuges) of Buddhism are to be found in the Buddha, the sangha and the dharma.

Buddha's Teaching

6

The Buddha taught in a conversational style rather than by lecturing. He encouraged questions and responded according to the understanding of the listener using everyday language, rather than the ancient Sanskrit used by Brahmin priests in their ceremonies. The texts written long after his death reveal his conversational style. He would make the same few points repeatedly in different ways according to the time, the place and the people. He is reported as saying:

> Now, I know well that when I approached various large assemblies, even before I sat down there or had spoken or began to teach, whatever was their sort I made myself of a like sort, whatever their language, so was my language. And I rejoiced them with a talk on dharma, made it acceptable to them, set them on fire and gladdened them.

> (*Digha-Nikaya*-ii-109)

The Buddha is often likened to a spiritual physician who first diagnoses the sickness, realizes that it can be cured and how, and then gives the right medicine to make the patient well. His teaching style was undoubtedly less formal than it must appear when described even in a book such as this.

Sometimes Buddhism is accused of negativity with its emphasis on suffering, but the opposite is the truth. The Buddha exemplified the joy of knowing an end to desires and suffering. He knew the solution to suffering and the causes of it. We are attached to how we think things should be and suffer when they are not. We resist accepting the loss of something we hold dear, and desire to possess or attain things we imagine will make us happy. Our greatest attachment is to the idea of an eternal self and this falsehood attracts inevitable suffering.

* Any desire causes suffering because what we have we cannot keep for ever, and we suffer in anticipating or experiencing that loss.

* We may not have everything we want, so inevitably we are disappointed, suffer longing and experience dissatisfaction.

* Our intentions, actions and decisions create suffering as a consequence. This is natural law (karma) because intentions of any kind assume intended future effects, which confirms one is attached to desires.

* The Eightfold Path is the means to liberate ourselves from desires and end suffering. Buddha taught this with certainty because he had experienced it and knew it to be true.

KARMA, DESIRES AND REBIRTH

According to the Buddha, we have certain characteristics that define us, whether we are human or animal. These are called **skandhas**, from the Sanskrit word meaning 'group' (also known as **aggregates**). The important, though unwelcome, truth which the Buddha insisted upon, was that there is no *self* residing in any of these characteristics, nor in the sum of them. A

> **KEYWORDS**
>
> **Skandhas:** Sanskrit word for 'group' or 'characteristics'.
>
> **Aggregates:** constituent elements collected together in a mass.

core self, or atman, would imply a fixed point of reference around which events centre, which the Buddha knew to be untrue. Everything is impermanent, and everything depends on an earlier cause. Nothing is eternal. All 'we' have is an impersonal stream of consciousness and this falsely creates an 'identity' from the sense impressions which seem to happen to 'me'. The Buddha understood how senses, one occurring after another, might create the impression of a self which is 'having' senses, but taught that there is no organizing principle behind the senses and sense organs.

As birth brings together the skandhas in a particular formation, so death dissipates them. There is only continuity inasmuch as past acts and intentions will play themselves out, if not in this life, then in another. There is no self or continuing core identity that can be reborn.

(Though the laws of karma cannot be detected by our senses, we are told the Buddha intuited their truth during the deep meditation of his enlightenment.)

The Buddha rejected **annihilationism** and **eternalism**. There is no possibility of an identity continuing when physical form, feelings, perceptions and mental formations are all impermanent. What would be the vehicle by which a 'self' entered another life when all these have perished? What aspect of a 'person' is unchanging enough to house a self even in this life?

The Buddha tried to make the difficult concept of rebirth without identity more easily understood by using everyday references. For example, a drop of water drawn from a mighty river may seem to have a separate existence or 'life'.

KEYWORDS

Annihilationism: the doctrine of no afterlife at all. Complete cessation at death.

Eternalism: at the time of the Buddha, this was belief in a self which survives death unchanged. Its meaning changed in Mahayanan Buddhism later.

Nirvana: the release of previously held false beliefs, leading to the end of desires and suffering. Freedom from rebirth.

If it is returned to the river and another drop is extracted, though the second is made of the same chemical constituents of water as the first there is no continuity of identity between these, nor any subsequent drops. Rebirth is similarly a reconstituting of elements without an eternal identity.

Any cravings which remain undissipated when the characteristics we assume to be 'me' die, flow into a new group of characteristics which will be neither the same as the old group, nor entirely different. The particular nature the next group of characteristics will take will depend on the nature of the unexpended karma remaining when the previous group of characteristics dissipated, or 'died'. In other words, the energy yet to be played out. There is no self to become annihilated, eternal or otherwise. Only freedom from craving and karma can prevent this onflowing, or rebirth from happening, and only **nirvana** – an ethical life and liberation from ignorance – will bring this freedom.

The Wheel of Becoming.

THE THREE CHARACTERISTICS OF EXISTENCE

The first teaching given by the Buddha was to the monks who had been with him during the years when he had practiced austerities. He explained the three interrelated characteristics which govern all existence.

1 All conditioned things are impermanent (Anicca)

Impermanence is a universal fact. It applies to humans, to ideas, thoughts and feelings, to animals, trees, mountains, rivers or any other thing we may name. Impermanence, or **Anicca** is an inescapable fact. We delude ourselves

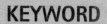

KEYWORD

Anicca: impermanence.

with the more comfortable notions of identity and permanence because we fear the thought of non-existence, yet the very fact of existence presupposes a natural cycle; a birth, which also presupposes eventual death and decay. All things are subject to constant change from moment to moment, and eventual decay and destruction. There is no self living through time, only a collection of ever-changing aggregates. The process of change may be fast and observable, or slow and seemingly hidden, but change and decay are universal laws of nature.

> **KEYWORDS**
>
> Dukkha: universal suffering.
>
> Anatta: non-self.

2 All living things suffer (Dukkha)

All thinking, feeling creatures resist and fear change, and cling to the comfort of the known. Death is our biggest fear because it is the greatest change we face, and as we know illness may lead to death, and ageing certainly does, we fear and resist these too. Only the process of life itself is continuous, manifesting in many, many forms. To become attached to any individual manifestation of life is a guarantee of future heartache and loss. We do not own the life which animates us any more than a candle owns the flame which gives the light. Suffering, or **dukkha**, is caused by a desire to fix or hold on to what must change, and to want what we cannot have. The sense impressions in themselves are not the cause of suffering. It is how we interpret them. Our desire for a sense of permanence, including the belief and desire for an eternal life, is counter to natural law. We doom ourselves to suffer by wanting the impossible and by resisting the unpleasant and the inevitable. Suffering is unsatisfactory and brings sorrow. Sorrow is unsatisfactory and brings suffering.

3 There is no self or eternal soul (Anatta)

The Buddha realized that impermanence is a universal law without exceptions. There can be no eternal soul or continuance of a fixed identity once the body which formerly held the grouped human characteristics decays and dies. We are also mistaken if we cling to the idea of having no-self, since to speak or think of an 'I' that has no self is still to hold an illusory belief dependent on identity. 'I have…' or 'I have not…' both presuppose the fallacy of a fixed identity which could possess or not possess anything.

CONSCIOUSNESS AND FALSE IDENTITY

Consciousness is the product of past karma, perhaps accumulated over many births, projected into the unique interactions of the present moment, and this is happening so seamlessly we may make the false assumption there is a stable identity that is experiencing change. On the contrary, there is no static identity, only change. No moment of consciousness can ever be recreated identically because this moment has different potential to any that has gone before.

The Buddha accepted that in everyday life we assume a personality for ourselves, and for what we perceive to be others, in order to function, even though in an absolute sense all life is just ever-changing groups of physical and mental aggregates. The illusion of personality is an easier concept although it has no corresponding reality. It is for the Buddhist to realize the fallacy of self-hood, identity and the idea of a soul, to escape endless rebirth. Life flows on, unchecked and unceasing, the energy passing to new physical aggregations on the death of the old until liberation from ignorance ends the chain. There is no death, though all forms that bear life die. There is just a change of direction until nirvana liberates us from the wheel of life altogether. It was with the realization and surrender to the implications of these truths that the Buddha was liberated from attachments and suffering and freed from rebirth.

KARMA

Karma simply means action, but can also mean work, tradition, or the spiritual law of cause and effect, according to the context in which the word is used. Karma, as described by the Buddha, is the law of non-judgemental and disinterested consequences, or more simply, the law of effects following from causes. Every intentional deed is like a seed. Births and deaths are but moments in an endless cycle. All living beings are links in this chain, not just human beings. Humans are more fortunate in having the intelligence to reach the spiritual understanding which ends karma for ever. Accumulated karma is not dissipated with the death of the aggregates we think of as the body. Consciousness seamlessly continues into another group of aggregates, which we call rebirth. Only complete experience of all the effects we initiated by our own intent will release us from the consequences of karma. That is complete nirvana such as the Buddha achieved at his death.

Translated, the word karma means 'action' or 'deed'. It does not, as it is so often mis-stated, mean 'fate'. According to the Buddha, existence is not governed by destiny or fate. Like a ripple from a pebble dropped into a lake, the effects created by our intentions will prevail until exhausted. An individual effect may cause a reaction with the effects created by our other intentions (ripples caused by other pebbles we dropped into the pond). These may interact to cause a reduction, or an increase, of the initial effect (enlarging or absorbing the first ripple). Karma arises equally from thoughts or speech as well as any physical acts. It is our intentions, present and past, even when initiated during previous births, which lead to consequences, whether or not the intent is physically enacted. The Buddha stressed that we are the agents of our own experience. So a basically good person may accumulate less karmic effect from the same action that will cause a basically corrupt person to suffer more.

We all suffer or enjoy the fruits of our own past intentional acts, so to envy or hate another, or to regret our luck, is pointless. What we may usefully do, however, is to follow the Eightfold Path, cultivate right attitudes and thereby create positive karma, and perhaps ultimately free ourselves from ignorance. We should accept the experiences which befall us in life as the effects of our own past actions. If one person lives a healthy life while another suffers illness, one lives long while another dies young, and so on, there is no divine judgement at work, simply cause and effect. Good (often called skilful) actions will lead to good consequences, and unskilful, or bad, actions will lead to bad consequences, each according to interaction with the effects of our other actions. The effects may be experienced in this birth, or may be in a future one.

We create our own suffering.

We are not determined by our past actions however – we have **free will**. We still have the freedom to act in ways that will counter-effect our past karma. There is no predestiny or **fate**. It is by our own freely chosen intentional actions that we improve on unhappy situations, or create our own future misery. A life skilfully and responsibly lived can alter one's next rebirth by the karma it will generate. Conduct that lessens attachment to the physical world lessens desires and will lead to a better birth next time the wheel turns. Attachments and desires will lead to a worse rebirth. The Buddha said, 'It is karma that differentiates beings into low and high states.' It is ignorance of this law that causes us to perpetuate our own suffering. The Buddha is quoted in the **Dharmapada** as saying that '...there is no hiding place for the man who has committed evil actions, not in the sky, in the ocean depths nor in a mountain cave. Neither will any of these places shield him from the inevitability of death'.

KEYWORDS

Free will: freedom to act. No predestiny to restrain action.

Fate: an unalterable, prederetmined future.

Dharmapada: an ancient collection of Buddhist verses that illustrate the dharma and the way to liberation.

Karma arises from good acts just as it does from bad ones. Although ethical intentions are sensible for our own sakes, as well as being of benefit to others, even good intentions if they are made in the expectation of good effects, are a barrier to liberation. Any and all intentional acts or desires will result in rebirth, and hinder liberation.

Karma is a natural law, not a moral one. Only when we are enlightened to the illusion of what we have formerly taken to be existence, and act in freedom from all desires and hatred, will we cease to create karmic effects and rebirth. It is of benefit to follow the Eightfold Path, even if we are not able to reach all the way to enlightenment in this birth.

DEPENDENT ORIGINATION

Indivisible from the law of karma is belief in **dependent origination**. This is the explanation given by the Buddha for how effects follow inevitably from causes. This is as important a concept as universal impermanence.

According to the Buddha each thing originates because of another thing that has preceded it. Material and mental events alike have causes, and this chain of becoming is constant. The law of dependent origination explains how some things seem to have permanence as though they were eternal, 'uncaused' and existing independently of other things, while others seem to be completely annihilated when destroyed. Dependent origination explains a middle way between these opposites. Things have existence but are not eternal. That we exist is not the illusion; that we are eternal and have a separate **core self** is. When we forget dependent origination, said the Buddha, we suffer, but recollection of its truth ends suffering.

Dependent origination was a means for the Buddha to teach his followers how they are the agents of their own fortune, and how the Eightfold Path offers a way to free themselves from suffering. His motives were compassionate, not scholarly, so though he knew from experience he did not dwell on explanations of concepts which were beyond words. He deflected unknowable metaphysical questions in favour of dealing with the obviously manifest, such as the existence of ignorance in the world, regardless of its cause.

The actual number of dependent originations listed by the Buddha varied in his different discourses on the subject, but generally twelve are held to encapsulate his teaching.

1 Ignorance

From ignorance arises suffering and the wheel of becoming. It produces a false sense of self or ego which clings to life. Ignorance separates us from the world and is the root of our actions.

2 Predispositions

From ignorance innate tendencies arise, which may be classed as good or bad. An innate tendency towards spiritual aspiration may give rise to a birth where opportunities for advancement arise. An innate tendency to desire wealth may cause rebirth in a wealthy family.

3 Consciousness

From intentional activities, consciousness arises. Consciousness remains after the death of the physical body, the senses and perceptions. From consciousness arises a new birth unless consciousness is ended with liberation (nirvana) at the point of death. Consciousness of self is the cause of rebirth.

4 Name and form

From consciousness arises names and forms. We are always conscious of something. If there were no sense of self there would be no objects for us to believe we are relative to. An object is a meaningless concept without relationship to a subject. They are interdependent.

5 Sensations

From names, forms and consciousness arise the six (Buddhist) sensations: sight, smell, taste, touch and mental activity.

6 Contact

From the six sensations arise the external organs with which contact with the outer world is made. The outer world arises from forms and ideas. From seeing arises eyes; from hearing arises ears; from aromas arises the nose; from taste arises the tongue; from touch arises the skin; from mental activity arises the mind.

7 Feeling

From contact with external things or mental activity arises feelings and emotions, such as pain, pleasure, love, hatred, likes and dislikes. Feelings and emotions create attachments or aversions to objects in the world.

8 Craving
From feelings and emotions cravings arise. We like some feelings and dislike others. Craving creates perceptions, the fifth aggregate, or skandha, one of the five constituents of manifestation, which cause further rebirth. Suffering disappears once cravings are overcome.

9 Attachment
From cravings arise attachments to ideas or objects in the world and how they seem to make us feel. Cravings create a sense of lack, which leads to suffering. We cling to our desires to have and to hold, or avoid and escape from; ideas, ideals and objects.

10 Being
From attachments arises being. Coming-to-be arises from the grouped constituents of being that are created by our attachments and cravings.

11 Rebirth
From being, or coming-to-be, arises actual rebirth into ignorance and another turn of the wheel of dharma from which only the realizations of nirvana can release us.

12 Ageing and death
From rebirth arises the suffering of worldly experience, sorrow, old age and death. From ignorance we accumulate the aggregations and karma which will endlessly cause more rebirths until we attain liberation from the Wheel of Becoming. Rebirth may occur in any of six realms, three pleasant and three unpleasant, according to the karmic accumulation. The human realm is regarded as one of the more pleasant because it offers an easier path to attaining nirvana than most others.

AGGREGATES (SKANDHAS)
So we see how each quality depends on and flows from its predecessor. No personal identity transfers from one life to another. Karma continues from birth to birth, in an uninterrupted stream of accumulated energy, so long as aggregates have been produced by the whole chain of dependent origination during life.

Aggregates (skandhas) are the attributes by which we recognize something. In the case of a human being, they are the group of characteristics that must be present for us to recognize what we perceive as a human being. Animals have similar aggregations which define our perception of them as beings which are not human. These characteristics do not define any core self such as is attributed to the human condition in other philosophies, because all these attributes are unfixed and constantly changing.

To have the appearance of what we take to be human, we will have the following ever-changing aggregates. None of these constitutes, or contributes to, what we falsely believe to be a self:

* material composition; physicality;
* senses, including mental impressions;
* perception;
* mental formations producing character;
* consciousness.

These five aggregate constituents change all the time. They do not singly or collectively amount to a core self and are not of themselves worthy of desire. To realize these truths is to realize that nothing in or of the world will bring happiness or sadness, and to realize that we are perfect and free.

Specific accumulated karmas condition the nature of the subsequent birth. Life is an impersonal and detached process, not the journey of an identity, self or soul from anywhere to anywhere. There is no being to enter anywhere at nirvana. Our present life is caused by our past lives, but our future life depends on what we make of the present life. There is no fixed destiny since we always have the free will to release ourselves from suffering. We are responsible for what we experience now and for what we do about it.

The Wheel of Suffering.

EFFORT AND PERSONAL ACHIEVEMENT

Buddhism as taught by the Buddha is unusual among religions in placing no reliance on outside forces, divine or ecclesiastic, for assistance. The Buddha taught that there was no expectation of intercession from any outside force. Supernatural intervention is not an option. There was no one to whom to appeal for assistance by means of prayer or supplication, and no substitute for personal responsibility and achievement. No god, divine grace, saint or spirit is available to help another individual to achieve liberation. That task remains for each person to achieve alone by means of personal effort, diligence and right living. It is questionable whether the teachings of the Buddha technically amount to a religion, with their absence of divine input. However, the fact that millions of people venerate the man who reintroduced the dharma into the world, and follow his teaching, is generally accepted as evidence enough.

Rituals and prayers cannot undo the laws of karma. A monk or nun may be inspired by the teaching and example of the Lord Buddha, but the effort must be his or her own. The Buddha showed his followers the way. He could not walk it for them. 'Be a lamp unto yourselves', was said to be his final advice.

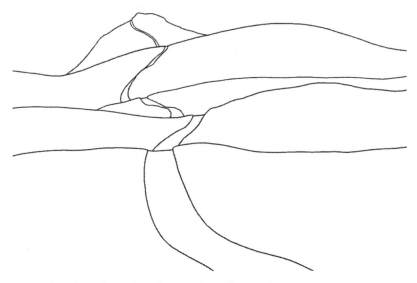

To travel on the path you must become the path.

TRUST, ETHICAL CONDUCT AND MEDITATION

The Buddha asked his followers to refrain from evil, to do good and to purify the mind, by identifying and eradicating imperfect thoughts. Inward concentration and meditation, trust in the dharma and adherence to **ethics** are the

KEYWORD

Ethics: set of moral principles.

keys to the Buddha's teaching. It is important to make time for quiet contemplation each day, to bring harmony and balance to life. It is easy to be deceived by sensory input into forgetting there is no self. Meditation and contemplation train the Buddhist to be awake and alert to this tendency. Through meditation the Buddhist should cultivate:

* knowledge of the dharma, which teaches control and compassion for oneself and for others caught in the web of suffering born of ignorance;

* high ethical standards in thought and action;
* detached contemplation of the body, the mind, the emotions and the sensations, of how they arise and pass.

Monks are encouraged to meditate upon death, to think about what feelings arise when it is contemplated, what is it that dies, and so on. Frequently the monk meditates before a skull or pile of bones to focus on the inevitability of death. With an ever-present awareness of death comes constant diligence to work harder, realize the truth and end the suffering of rebirth.

The Buddha acknowledged that rules should not be adhered to slavishly if a higher ethical course may be served by ignoring them. The wisdom to discriminate and act ethically is a personal responsibility to be reassessed in each moment. Ethics have always been at the heart of Buddhist practice.

REBIRTH

In the *Dharmapada* the Buddha likens life to a house, which is built and rebuilt time and again, to explain rebirth. He is reputed to have told listeners how he had searched so long for the builder of this house of life, through the cycles of many lives and deaths, and now at last he had seen the housebuilder. This house would never be rebuilt again because the rafters of past bad actions had been broken, the ridge-pole of ignorance destroyed, and his fever of cravings was over.

Early Buddhists thought there could be only one Buddha alive at any time, because according to the teaching, a Buddha-to-be is reborn to live a final life only when the world has forgotten the dharma taught by the previous one. Therefore, once a Buddha had appeared, if any

KEYWORD

Arhant (Arhat): one who has gained insight into the true nature of things.

other people gained insight into the dharma and became perfected in their behaviour and understanding, they were called **Arhants** (**Arhats**). Such people had reached the penultimate stage of enlightenment, and would gain a conditional and partial liberation, with a better rebirth according to their remaining karma. Arhants attained non-attachment in this life only. Later Buddhists did not limit the experience of full nirvana to the Buddha of the age. During this life the senses still function, even after becoming an arhant. There is neither attachment to pleasurable senses nor rejection of unpleasant ones. Rebirth is caused by karma, cravings and aversions still present in consciousness at the death of (the aggregates we know as) a physical body. If at physical death all sense of possession and craving has ceased, there is no latency to promote another birth.

NIRVANA

Enlightenment, or nirvana, has been described as reaching the understanding that there is no self or soul, and nothing (such as a god) with which to achieve union at the death of the physical body. No desires or attachments remain, since it is beyond reason to hold them in the face of this truth. Neither priests nor god(s) can bestow nirvana and sacrifices are not part of the process. It is rare for a human to achieve this level of detachment and insight. Once the truth has been realized and surrendered to, the end of that person's life is like a flame which has been blown out, according to the Buddha. The flame does not go anywhere. Where would it have been before it was here and where would it go to next? Complete and total nirvana such as this is so rare that, at the time when Siddhartha lived, it was thought to occur only on the death of a Buddha. Nirvana confers a complete escape from rebirth, because no attachments or karma remain.

The Buddha wisely discouraged questions regarding nirvana, realizing that any answers he might give would be taken as definitive. Definitions create mental expectations, mental expectations create attachments, and mental attachments would then also have to be overcome by the aspirant. Even the teaching must be interpreted according to the situation with ethical understanding and not as an inflexible set of rules. nirvana is impossible to describe adequately since the concept cannot be contained or expressed by language. Any verbal definition would suggest artificial and exclusive boundaries, yet nirvana is beyond the dualities of 'is' or 'is not'. Nirvana must be known, not described. Nonetheless attempts have been made.

Nirvana is often described in negatives. It is however as impossible to exclude as it is to include all that it is. The Buddha repudiated the idea that nirvana is the extinguishing of anything, since that would imply the existence of a self that could become extinguished. Rather it is the letting go of previously held false beliefs. All that might be said to be extinguished is any desire for rebirth, or clinging to notions of permanence, since one who knows realizes there is no lasting identity or self for which future desires could be appropriate. Psycho-physical death cannot touch the person who achieves nirvana, because such a person dies to each moment. Such a one acts disinterestedly, without desire for a particular outcome, and without identifying a self with the action. Indeed, such a person knows that there is no self who is the doer or who can die. Belief in a self is part of the illusion, though a most seductive part.

We naturally want to know and be known by others and to believe that in some form we live for ever. All these desires are doomed to failure since they rest upon a basic misconception about *what is*. Nothing is permanent in the universe, least of all what we take to be ourselves. Everything is in motion, everything changes. It is illusory to imagine identity.

Surrender to the experience of nirvana brings peace and causes the dissolution of hatred, greed and any delusions of an enduring essence. The awakening brings the realization that flux, or change, is the natural state of the whole universe. There is therefore no sense in clinging to the notion of a permanent existence, when in truth such a state does not exist anywhere, or in anything, least of all in our lives. (The Buddha emphasized that suicide is not an acceptable option either, since it creates bad karma and causes rebirth.)

Nirvana is the only hope of escape from the wheel of rebirth to which we are tied by our actions, whether for good or ill. We set the wheel to spin and wonder why we cannot get off, when all the while we are giving it another push. The death of the Buddha's physical body marked his last life, since with his understanding and exemplary life, no karma remained to cause a rebirth.

SUMMARY

- The Buddha stated there is no enduring self, essence or atman.

- The three characteristics of existence, according to the Buddha, are impermanence, suffering and no-self.

- Dependent origination was the Buddha's way to explain the chain of illusions that cause us to believe in an enduring identity or eternal self.

- The experience of nirvana gives release from suffering and rebirth.

Early Buddhism

THE PREVAILING ORAL TRADITION

It was a long established tradition for religious teaching and moral tales to be passed on by word of mouth. Few could read or write the ancient Sanskrit language of the *Vedic* texts used by the Brahmins. The oral tradition was so well established and popular that listeners to the stories knew them by heart, as well as the storytellers who travelled from village to village telling them. When the life and teaching of the Buddha was memorized by those who had heard him teach, this method was neither unusual nor likely to be inaccurate.

THE TEN ETHICAL PRECEPTS

To be ordained in a Buddhist order it was necessary to undertake ten promises, or precepts. Lay members, who did not renounce ordinary life only undertook to keep the first five.

1 Abstain from killing.
2 Abstain from stealing.
3 Abstain from improper sexual conduct.
4 Abstain from lying, improper thoughts or speech.
5 Abstain from using intoxicants.
6 Abstain from eating other than at prescribed times.
7 Abstain from singing and dancing.
8 Abstain from using cosmetics.
9 Abstain from sleeping on a comfortable bed.
10 Abstain from accepting gifts of gold or silver.

THE ABSENCE OF CLASS OR CASTE DISTINCTIONS

The Buddha taught the dharma to anyone who wanted to hear it – to men and women of any caste, any occupation and any religion. He taught that freedom from an endless cycle of birth and suffering was possible for anyone aware of the truth. There should be no ranks or castes among the monks and nuns; all are equal in dharma. To this end he said there should be no social divisions within the sangha.

Most of the questions Brahmin priests asked of the Buddha as he travelled from village to village were demands that he acknowledge their right to preserve their status, rather than philosophical or religious debates. The Buddha was accused by them of encouraging self-centredness by offering an individual path to spiritual advancement. If the Eightfold Path did all that the Buddha claimed it would only benefit one person, whereas the Brahmins said, priestly practices benefit many people at once.

The *Pali Canon* includes many derogatory references to Brahmins (probably later commentaries) which accuse them of greed and exploitation, and ascribe many vices to them. Animal sacrifices had become widespread and were a lucrative source of income for the priests who alone had the correct status to perform them.

The Buddha is recorded as having taught his listeners to judge others by their actions, not by their class. In a **sutra** (a sacred text) he is quoted as saying: 'Not by birth is one an outcaste. Not by birth is one a Brahmin. By deed one

> **KEYWORD**
>
> Sutra: Buddhist doctrinal text or scripture.

becomes an outcaste. By deed one becomes a Brahmin.' The Buddha named five well-known rivers. He told his listeners that despite being so large and famous, each loses its separate identity once its waters pour out into the ocean. Just so for all who join the sangha, regardless of their former status. Examples like this helped listeners to realize the error of attaching importance to class or status.

BECOMING A BUDDHIST MONK

The Buddha ordained the first monks himself, granting permission for them to leave their homes and join the order. Ordination was by a simple command to come and hear the dharma and make an end to anguish. As monks began to travel the country they ordained suitable candidates by shaving the candidate's head, the wearing of the distinctive yellow robe, and by hearing a declaration of the Three Jewels of Buddhism.

* I take refuge in the Buddha.
* I take refuge in the dharma.
* I take refuge in the sangha (the community of monks).

The Buddha encouraged would-be initiates to leave their homes and traditional Brahmanic roles in order to devote their future lives to the search for personal truth. They would henceforth live within the protective community of the sangha, rather than the household, and would forsake their former religious rituals and family expectations.

BECOMING A BUDDHIST NUN

Nuns were somewhat reluctantly ordained by the Buddha, when he had to agree they could equally well achieve liberation. We may suppose he feared the presence of women might have a negative effect on the social cohesion of a celibate order. Whatever the reason, nuns were required to obey more restrictive rules than monks, and to show more respect to a monk than a monk was required to do to a nun, regardless of how senior or established the nun, and how junior or new the monk.

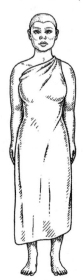

All Buddhists are equal but some Buddhists are more equal than others.

Eventually separate orders of nuns were developed. They lived apart from monks, though both sexes sought the same spiritual ideals. Later, falling numbers of nuns caused the dissolution of these separate orders, which eventually led to the complete cessation of the ordination of women. Women still joined the order, but were not now ordained or given the same status as formerly. The authentic ordination of Theravada nuns ended officially in AD 456 though modern Buddhist orders, particularly in America, admit nuns. In other countries today women may join a sangha where though important, they remain subordinate and are not ordained.

THE ROLE OF THE LAITY

Monks had food supplied by the laity, the people among whom they lived. It was and is the traditional practice in South Asia for food and material goods to be given to spiritual wanderers in the hope and belief that merit, or good karma, would accrue to the giver. The sight of monks or spiritual seekers regularly begging for their daily food was therefore not at all unusual. Gifts to the monks and nuns might include robes (or the material with which to make them), food, medicine, or shelter in the case of a travelling monk.

Today the sangha may be taken to mean all those who follow the Buddhist path – monks, nuns and laity – but originally it referred only to ordained monks and nuns. All the rules and regulations governing the sangha were devised for the monks, and later the nuns, by the Buddha in person. He showed great understanding of how tensions and disagreements could arise if not anticipated. The laity were not subject to organizational restrictions but were expected to try to live according to Buddhist ideals.

The early monks were allowed only a few possessions: a robe, a belt, a needle, a begging bowl, a toothpick, a razor, a staff or walking-stick, and a filter for drinking water. Buddhist monks today have a few more possessions, such as an umbrella and an anorak perhaps, but still only as many things as are personally essential. The laity are still an essential aspect of the successful functioning of a monastery. The monks play a reciprocal function in providing access to the dharma, in attending to the ceremonial needs of the lay members, as at funerals and celebrations, and in keeping alive the ancient texts. In giving an opportunity for the laity to be generous, the monks also give them the chance to create good karma.

PRAYER AND WORSHIP

The Buddha had always deflected personal attention away from himself to the dharma. Right action and understanding would lead to liberation and the end of karma, not attachment to a man, nor to prayer and rituals. His teaching always centred on practical action, not on religiosity. The first Buddhist monks were required to serve the wider community and spread the truth in any way possible through compassion for the plight of all sentient beings. They were not to keep themselves apart in an elitist manner.

The Buddha's followers were taught there is no god whom they might worship, or to whom they might pray for intercession in their lives. However, the habit of worship and prayer was so much a part of the religious and cultural tradition of India that aspects of the traditional ways were gradually reinstated after the Buddha's death. However, what might look like worship was actually veneration. His followers were expressing their gratitude, devotion and awe for the achievements of a great teacher, not expecting him to act as a saviour from beyond the grave.

So the early Buddhists venerated the Buddha but would not have expected him to intercede in any way. He was a man who had escaped rebirth, not a supernatural being. Relics of the Buddha, and any traces of his life were venerated as reminders of spiritual aspiration, not prayed to as if the Buddha were a god or would in any way receive the veneration personally. Even statues of the Buddha's likeness were discouraged for a long time after his death. The Buddha had stressed, even as he was dying, that each person's path should be their own so to worship the physical form of the Buddha, or try to live an imitation of his earthly life, would not help anyone else with the path they must tread according to their own karma. **Statuary** was later introduced as a focus for respect. The Theravada school of Buddhism still holds to these beliefs.

Later schools of Buddhism, such as the Mahayana school, reinterpreted the Buddha's teaching. Liberation was said to be available to everyone without leaving their everyday life while the monks kept themselves and some aspects of the teaching, such as meditation techniques, apart. The Buddha was also reinterpreted as a supernatural being who continues to look on the world with compassion from beyond the grave, who is present in all the realms of existence into which karma may cause rebirth, and whose protection can be sought and received. The help of large numbers of Bodhisattvas (here meaning enlightened beings) is also sought through prayer and worship at shrines. Even key religious texts are worshipped as part of Mahayana Buddhist practice.

> # KEYWORDS
>
> **Statuary:** statues of the presumed likeness of the Buddha.
>
> **Bodhi tree:** tree under which the Buddha achieved enlightenment.
>
> **Stupa:** a memorial mound or structure to the Buddha or other enlightened being.
>
> **Relics:** human remains or artifacts connected with a venerated person.

THE MONASTERY

The first followers of the Buddha became wandering holy men living the same austere life that he had, relying on alms for food. In the rainy season, when these wanderers needed shelter, they would build a vihara (monastery). The first monasteries were simple shelters, but in time they became permanent centres. They usually comprised of a walled compound within which were gardens and simple dwellings for monks. It was common to have a **Bodhi tree** within the grounds, and sometimes they would be built around or near a **stupa** which might or might not contain **relics**. There would have been no images of the Buddha within the first monasteries. The monastery would serve the spiritual needs of the lay community and receive alms from them.

✳ ✳ ✳ ✳SUMMARY ✳ ✳ ✳ ✳

• In ancient times, few people could read and fewer still had the means to write, so religious teaching was always learned by heart and passed on orally.

• All Buddhists promise not to kill, steal, lie (or have improper thoughts), engage in improper sexual conduct, or take intoxicants.

• Monks and nuns also promise to eat only at prescribed times, not to sing or dance, not to use cosmetics, not to sleep on a comfortable high bed, and not to accept gold, silver or otherwise deal with money.

• Somewhat reluctantly the Buddha stated that women can also achieve nirvana.

• The Buddha set up a sangha (community) to help Buddhist seekers after truth.

Death

THE BUDDHA'S ILLNESS AND DEATH

The Buddha knew that his health and vitality were fading, yet worked even harder to teach as many people as he could before his death. His journeys had taken him to the region we know today as Patna, in northeast India, where he reminded an assembled crowd of the benefits of ethical behaviour and the Eightfold Path. He then went with Ananda, his cousin, to Venugrama (the Bamboo village) where he meant to retreat until the rainy season was over. He told Ananda the sangha must rely on the dharma as their teacher after his death, which he sensed was not far away.

His health was failing, but once the rains eased he travelled on to Vaisali. There he told monks who came to see him they should practice the dharma so the teaching would survive him. Again he travelled on through villages in the northeast. In one of these villages he is said to have received the meal that precipitated his death. The many dishes served in his honour aggravated a digestive complaint the Buddha had endured for a long time. Despite his discomfort, the Buddha thanked the giver of the feast and set out on the road again, bound now for Kusinagara (today known as Kasia in Uttar Pradesh). He and Ananda stopped at a grove of trees when the Buddha could go no further. He asked Ananda to make him a bed between two trees on which he lay, fully conscious, on his right side, with his head to the north and his face to the west. He taught during the night, and comforted those who gathered as he lay there. Ananda was particularly upset at the thought of his master reaching his final nirvana in such a lowly spot. The Buddha compassionately reassured him that it was actually an auspicious site from one of his former births, and that with so many loyal disciples nearby it was an excellent place.

The Buddha promised Ananda that he would reach the understanding of an arhant in this life. Ananda asked if the Buddha would tell them who his successor should be. He replied:

> As I have never sought to direct or subject the community to my teachings, I leave no such instruction to the sangha. I am reaching my end. After my death each of you will be your own island, your own refuge. Take no other refuge.
>
> (*Digha-Nikaya*, ii, 100)

The dharma itself was to be the Buddha's successor.

THE FINAL NIRVANA

Local people learning that the great Lord Buddha would reach his final nirvana nearby flocked to see him and pay their respects. Subhadra, an ascetic, wanted to ask the Buddha many questions and would not be dissuaded by Ananda, who tried to protect his master from strain. The Buddha taught Subhadra, converting and ordaining him into the sangha, without consideration for his own health. The Master reiterated his most important teachings and encouraged questions from the disciples present, but all remained silent. When Ananda became upset at his teacher's imminent death, the Buddha consoled him with the words: 'Do not weep. It is in the nature of things that we part from what we hold most dear, so why be upset?' He then uttered his last words: 'All component things are perishable. Work diligently on your own salvation – be a lamp unto yourself.'

The Buddha meditated on throughout the night. He reached a level of super-consciousness in which all thoughts and feelings cease and material considerations are transcended. He then died peacefully. There were no karmic effects or attachments remaining to cause his rebirth in order for them to be played out. The Buddha had achieved final nirvana free from rebirth on the full moon day of July, aged 80, having taught for 45 years.

THE FUNERAL

The funeral of the Buddha was not organized by the Buddha's monks. The local people, the Mallas, conducted it in accordance with Indian funeral traditions.

The Buddha's body was washed and bathed with oil and then wrapped in the finest shrouds to be carried to the burning ground in a metal coffin. Legend tells us, however, that once there the **pyre** could not be lit. Hindu tradition dictated a cremation should be initiated by the

KEYWORD

Pyre: pile of combustible material for the cremation of a corpse.

eldest son (to have no male child was regarded as a great misfortune, since the proper rituals for one's funeral would be impossible). Mahakasypa, the Buddha's closest disciple, had been summoned from afar with news of the Buddha's death to assume this role. Mahakasypa wanted to kiss the feet of his revered teacher, a tradition still practiced today in Asia. It is said that the binding covering the Buddha's feet spontaneously unravelled, permitting his wish. Some legends say the funeral pyre spontaneously burst into flame and extinguished itself after the cremation without need of human intervention. Celebrations of music and dancing, with elaborate processions and offerings of perfume and flowers continued for a full week, in the manner of a royal funeral.

THE DISTRIBUTION OF HIS RELICS

In accordance with normal cremation practices, the charred bones and ashes of the Buddha's body were collected. Even coals from the funeral pyre and the vessel used to contain the bones became relics, but disputes arose over who should own them. The Mallas people wanted the relics as the Buddha had died in their territory and they had arranged the funeral, but powerful leaders from other regions also wanted to claim them. The Buddha's teaching concerning desires seemingly forgotten, his relics became highly desirable, sacred, and potentially powerful possessions. Powerful because possession of such relics might be taken to imply the approval of the Buddha himself, since surely they could not reside in the wrong hands. Reason prevailed on the brink of battle. By dividing the relics, all the contenders were satisfied. Monuments were erected over each relic which became places of pilgrimage and veneration.

THE CREATION OF TEMPLES

Temples were erected to house particularly venerated relics, or on the spot where a momentous event had occurred in the Buddha's life. Later they were also erected to celebrate the lives of other enlightened beings – Bodhisattvas and Arhants – and in honour of the former lives of the Buddha. These temples may be the base for a community of monks, but also serve the needs of local non-ordained Buddhists, the laity. Within the temple, as in a monastery, the dharma of the Buddha is kept alive.

THE HOLY SITES

Stupas are shrines or ancient holy places. Many of these monuments pre-dated Buddhism, but were used to contain relics of the Buddha or other important Buddhists such as his closest followers, the arhants.

The stupa at Sarnath, the site of the Buddha's first sermon.

Others were erected to commemorate acts in the Buddha's life, or previous lives. Over the centuries many monks and nuns sought to have their remains deposited near to those of the Buddha or other principle figures, a desire which suggests they had not achieved the wisdom of liberation. Hundreds of small stupas were erected around monastic centres, each engraved with the name of the individual whose ashes they contained.

Buddhists walk around the perimeter of a stupa or venerated object in a clockwise direction as an act of respect. They make offerings of flowers to honour the memory of the person connected with the site. The Bodhgaya, the bodhi tree under which the Buddha came to realize enlightenment, is a major site of pilgrimage. Many other trees have been grown from seeds or cuttings from the parent tree and these are also venerated.

* * * *SUMMARY* * * *

● The dying Buddha advised his listeners to work diligently on their own salvation and be a lamp unto themselves.

● Arhants (those who have attained enlightenment) are still subject to rebirth but are freed from desires and suffering in this life.

● The Buddha refused to appoint any successor other than the dharma (teaching).

● The Buddha deflected interest in himself back to the teaching. Temples and stupas which house sacred relics reflect the human need to worship.

9 Texts and Scriptures

LANGUAGE AND THE SCRIPTURES

The oral tradition was well developed at the time of the Buddha as few people could read and fewer still had the means to write. Added to this, Hindu religious texts tended to be in ancient languages other than those of everyday speech, so only priests who learned these languages could refer to them directly. To keep the principles of religious thought alive and share them, the religious stories and rules for daily conduct were learned by heart and recited. These recitations were a popular dramatic entertainment in village life as well as a chance to learn ethical principles from the example of characters within the tales. Once Buddhist monasteries were created, the practice of memorizing and reciting religious ideals continued, with monks and, later, nuns learning Buddhist teaching. The sangha thus served to reinforce and reaffirm the dharma, and to transmit it to any new members of the community.

Missionary monks brought Buddhism to Sri Lanka hundreds of years after the Buddha's death. The *Pali Canon* is so called because the scriptures were compiled in Sri Lanka using the Pali language. Pali was the language of everyday speech whereas Brahmanic texts were written in an ancient Sanskrit language no longer spoken and only read by scholars and priests. Pali, as a spoken language, could be written in any script which made it easily transmitted to different regions and countries.

The *Pali Canon*, as the collected texts are called, were written from memory of the original teachings which had passed down by word of mouth since the Buddha lived. Buddhist councils had agreed on the authentic versions from the various sources where the oral tradition had spread. Some scholars believe the *Pali Canon* is the elaboration of the originally more succinct teaching of the Buddha, others that it is an accurate transmission of the actual teaching.

The *Pali Canon* texts form the basis of the **Theravada** school of Buddhism, which was one of many that developed after the death of the Buddha. Mahayana Buddhism, which arose from a schism over the teaching, has developed along different lines. Both schools, and others which came later, have no problem in acknowledging that all are Buddhists however.

Mahayana Buddhist texts were recorded in Sanskrit, and suffered losses from the political upheavals, invasions, and translations from and to the native languages where Buddhism spread. The *Pali Canon* of South Asian origin remained largely intact. Today there are huge amounts of scriptural texts and other literature translated into many languages in both of the major schools of Buddhism.

KEYWORDS

Theravada: school of Buddhism that remains true to the earliest Buddhist doctrine.

Sutta: text containing sermons given by the Buddha himself or his close disciples.

Vinaya: text dictating the rules of the sangha as set up by the Buddha himself.

Buddha Vacana: the two texts (*Sutta* and *Vinaya*) that record the Buddha's own words

Abhidharma: Buddhist philosophy and later comments on the doctrine.

THE FIRST BUDDHIST SCRIPTURES

The earliest Buddhist scriptures were the doctrine (*Sutta*) and the rules governing monastic discipline (*Vinaya*). These two documents are reputed to have been the actual record of the Buddha's remarks (*Buddha Vacana*). Later a third collection of metaphysical speculations was added (*Abhidharma*).

The *Pali Canon*: The Triple Basket

This primary collection of texts, known as *Tripitaka*, was still not recorded until long after the death of the Buddha. 'Triple Basket' refers to the fact that when they were written (on palm leaves) in the Pali language, they were collected into bundles and stored in three baskets. The three baskets contain: the sermons of the Buddha and other key figures in early Buddhism (*Sutta*); the conduct to be adhered to by members of the Buddhist order (*Vinaya*); and the metaphysics and later analyses (*Abhidharma*). The texts were all bundled according to their content, and collectively known as the *Pali Canon*. Of all the texts, the one thought most important now is the *Sutta Pitaka* which contains the sermons, but immediately after the Buddha's death, the *Vinaya* – the rules Buddha had set out for the sangha – were thought to be the most important.

A text called the *Buddhavamsa* describes the lineage of the Buddha from the first of the 24 previous Buddhas to the next awaited, the Maitreya. The teaching of each Buddha would have been the same since the dharma – or truth – is eternal. Each Buddha is said to have appeared in the world when the teaching of his predecessor had ceased to be effective. Mankind loses sight of the dharma periodically, perhaps because the numbers of followers dwindle for whatever reason, to the point where the teaching is not passed on any more. Then the next Buddha-to-be will be born.

The *Jataka Tales*

The stories of the previous lives of the Buddha are recorded in the *Jataka Tales*. This collection of fabulous tales relates his actions in past lives when he was born in many different forms. The Buddha is said to have had experience of life as various animals, as well as his many previous human lives, both male and female. Many of the tales have been the subject of artistic interpretations in wall paintings, statuary and carvings. The *Jataka Tales* are still extremely popular with the young and old alike.

The *Dharmapada*

The *Dharmapada* (or *Dhammapada*), which translated means 'verses on the law', is one of the most beautiful and valued of Buddhist texts. It is the essence of the Buddha's teaching as compiled in the third century BC. The *Dharmapada* takes the form of a highly readable and inspirational collection of verses on the doctrine. The 423 verses or aphorisms are arranged under subject headings such as 'good and evil', 'mind', and 'cravings'. These verses teach Buddhist morals and the path to nirvana in an appealing format. The *Dharmapada* was incorporated into the *Pali Canon* in the collection of sermons of the Buddha. It has been translated into many languages and is still widely studied and enjoyed for its wisdom by Buddhists and non-Buddhists alike.

* * * *SUMMARY* * * *

● The 'Triple Basket' is another name for the *Pali Canon*. These are the earliest texts, recorded on bundles of palm leaves which were sorted into three baskets.

● Pali is unusual in being a spoken language that is written in the script forms of many other languages.

● The *Abhidharma* are later commentaries and metaphysical speculations on the earlier teaching.

● The Maitreya Buddha is stated to be the next Buddha who will renew the dharma.

10 Meditation and Contemplation

MEDITATION AND CONTEMPLATION

'Our life is shaped by our mind; we become what we think', said the Buddha. Meditation is a vital component of Buddhist practice, to be developed in conjunction with inner discipline and morality. The word 'meditation' is an approximate translation of the Pali word *bhavana*, which means 'the cultivation and development of the mind'. It is one of the steps in the Eightfold Path which the Buddha taught and one of the reasons why monks would leave their homes to join the sangha where they could regularly meditate for long hours, free from distractions.

Meditation leads to a calming of the mind and greater awareness and experience of the present moment. It is the means of learning to achieve clarity so that true reality may be perceived. The Buddha taught:

* in the seeing there should be just the seeing;
* in the hearing there should be just the hearing;
* and in the thinking there should be just the thought.

Then we see the world as it is, without prejudgement or prejudice. In our normal mental states we become obsessed with mind chatter, which obscures the simplicity of direct perception. We worry and plan for the future and mull over past events to the point that we are no longer present now. Yet all we have is now; this moment.

Meditation may be practiced by remaining alert and mindful throughout the normal activities of the day, or by sitting or walking in an attitude of silent, inner communion. Meditation today is usually taught by a more experienced Buddhist who monitors progress. It is usual to begin meditation with focused awareness on the breath as it enters and leaves the body, followed by concentration on a particular aspect of the teaching, such as impermanence, compassion or death. The Buddhist learns to contemplate a particular thought in this way, free from preconceptions. Topics such as a flame, a colour or a flower may be selected for attention by the teacher. As thoughts arise, the meditator considers who is the thinker, and questions each sensation in this way until it becomes evident that the 'I' of identity is an illusion. It takes patience, effort and practice.

The mind is gently taught to focus without forcing out irrelevant thoughts as they arise. All thoughts are observed, and allowed to pass until the monk finds only the one thought, sight, or other sense is operating within a calm and expanded mind freed from the usual mental chatter. Now he truly sees what is before him (or experiences whichever sense is operating), rather than carelessly accepting past knowledge and future expectation without being mentally present. He or she *knows* flame or flower, for example. As long as we invent our perceptions from historic imagining we cannot perceive the real.

Practice

* The meditator learns to sit erect and motionless, with the chest, neck and head erect and legs crossed. (The right foot is on the left thigh, and the left foot is on the right thigh. The soles of the feet face upwards, the hands resting on the thighs, and the palms turned upward.) This posture is usually called the 'lotus' position and has been found depicted on artifacts as ancient as the third millennium BC. With practice it is possible to remain relaxed but alert for long periods in this posture.

* The meditator fixes attention on the tip of his or her nose and observes the breath as it enters and leaves the body. The breath is not deliberately altered, but gradually it will become slower.

* Attention is turned within, until outer disturbances are no longer heeded. Peaceful contentment and serenity arise.

* Attention may now be brought to a single theme or object of contemplation upon which it remains calmly focused, noting without interference thoughts and feelings as they arise.

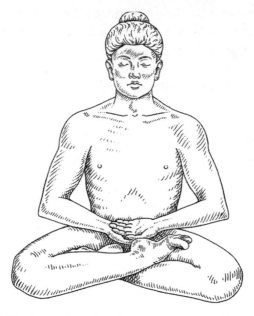

The lotus position is a traditional meditation posture in Buddhism.

* Attention may deepen to become **dhyana**, when awareness of mental activity is stilled completely to be replaced with pure presence; a state of poised indifference.

* Lastly, **samadhi** occurs. This is a loss of all sense of separateness between observer and observed, thinker and thought. True reality is experienced but all recollections of the experience are eliminated because perceptions are totally absent.

KEYWORDS

Dhyana: meditative state of concentration.

Samadhi: a deep state of meditation and altered awareness.

PLANES OF EXISTENCE AND STATES OF AWARENESS

The Buddha avoided answering questions about the various states of awareness to be experienced in meditation. To state them would raise expectations and thoughts which would act as a barrier to the meditative process. He is reputed to have stated that such questions are of no interest to anyone who has achieved deep meditative states. Nonetheless, there have been many speculations and attempts to describe the experience. Some declare the experience to be a positive fullness, while others say it is negative emptiness. Neither really conveys what has to be experienced rather than described.

❋ ❋ ❋ ❋*SUMMARY* ❋ ❋ ❋ ❋

● Meditation is a vital aspect of Buddhist practice.

● The Buddhist meditator is required to assume an erect posture when sitting cross-legged. Novices are supervised by a monk.

● The Buddha declined to explain what altered states of consciousness might occur through meditation because expectations are counter-productive to personal discovery.

Buddhist Cosmology

THE BUDDHIST EXPLANATION OF THE UNIVERSE

Complicated traditional ideas about the existence of other worlds and realms in the universe, and the beings who populate them, are part of Asian cultural history. These fabulous beings and other realms are mentioned in the *Jataka Tales* and have become part of Buddhist lore.

ANIMALS AND OTHER FABULOUS CREATURES

All animals are treated with respect and compassion in Buddhism, whether great or small, beneficial or harmful to man. All are bearers of consciousness and should not be harmed in any way and certainly should not be sacrificed. To this end, most Buddhists are vegetarians and would not undertake an occupation which causes animals to suffer in any way.

The Buddha rarely answered questions concerning the existence of spirits or demons, heavens and hells, saying that such speculation would not help the seeker advance towards enlightenment. When the senses have disappeared at death, it is pointless to wonder what might be known thereafter, or indeed how it could be known. Speculation is pointless. The Buddha reminded his questioners that it is quite enough to tackle the task of enlightenment without considering irrelevancies.

Although the Buddha rarely answered metaphysical questions, it seems he chose not to dispute the prevailing beliefs either. In the absence of teaching to the contrary, the ideas continued and became interwoven with the Buddha's own teaching, especially with the more legendary and supernatural stories which emerged concerning the lives of the Buddha. The early Buddhists had been brought up in a society where heavens and hells, gods, goddesses and demons were commonplace. Much of this traditional lore was maintained by the later schools of Buddhism which continue to accept these fabulous realms and mythological beings.

The ancient metaphysical explanations told of a multi-layered universe. A dozen or so groups of radiant beings, or **devas**, were said to live at the highest point above the earth. Below these, but still above the earth, lived four groups of gods of bliss, and beneath these resided the four groups of gods of light. At the lowest point, and nearest to the earth, were seven minor spiritual groups, the lesser devas. The earth itself was said to be disc-shaped with a great mountain at its centre surrounded by water. The earth was thought to be divided into four continents surrounded by four seas. Below the earth more realms were said to exist. Here the **asuras** or **titans** were condemned to live for failing in their attempt to take over the power of the gods. Lowest of all were the seven hells, each more terrifying than the last. Demons exist there and prey upon any whose karma causes rebirth into this sphere, at least until karma dictates another rebirth. Each of these layers was also said to have various spiritual components.

KEYWORDS

Devas: godlings, gods or radiant beings who have been reborn into one of the superior levels of being, having almost achieved enlightenment in a past life. They are also subject to the same laws of transience as afflict all sentient creatures, though they have a longer and a happier life than humans do. They are also subject to the wheel of rebirth until they become fully enlightened to the truth.

Asuras (titans): spirits who work sometimes for and sometimes against the gods. In the Buddhist cosmology they occupy a lower position than the earth. They seek power and are often depicted at war with the devas.

Nagas: are divine serpents which can take human form, or appear sometimes as half snake, half man. They are known to have symbolised water and fertility in Indian religions since Neolithic times. A famous tale describes how a naga protected the newly enlightened Buddha from inclement weather as he sat in deep meditation.

THE SYMBOLISM OF THE WHEEL

The wheel was a familiar image in ancient India where in Vedic and Hindu rituals it represented cosmic law and order. It symbolized the natural cycle of birth and death, as determined according to the law of karma. It is said that once started, no power can stop the wheel of life.

At times the wheel was used to signify the sun, itself the subject of ancient worship. It also represented the king's chariot wheel as an emblem of his power over ordinary individuals. In early Buddhist texts the Buddha was sometimes depicted or described as driving his chariot and claiming sovereignty over all the earth, like a king of the Vedic period. The wheel had other ancient meanings but has become known worldwide as a symbol of the Buddha's teaching today.

The Buddhist Wheel of the Law represents the dharma, the teaching. It was set in motion again by the Buddha Gautama, Buddha for this age, with his first sermon at the deer park. The wheel signifies to Buddhists:

* dependent origination – the essential part of the process of re-becoming described by the Buddha. This describes how every effect follows from a prior cause;

* the Eightfold Path – if the wheel is shown with eight spokes;

* the Buddha's authority and right to rule – if the wheel has numerous spokes;

* the cycle of rebirth – subject to karma.

Often a wheel is shown on the Buddha's hands or feet in Buddhist paintings and statuary. Sometimes it is above an empty throne with deer on either side. This reminds Buddhists of the power of the law (the throne) and the deer park where the Buddha preached his first sermon which started the wheel of dharma turning for this age.

All symbolic representations of aspects of the Buddha's teaching, such as the wheel, serve as a reminder it is the law which should be followed, and not the teacher of the law.

WOMEN AND BUDDHISM

Women in ancient Asia were generally subservient to men, in particular to their husbands. If widowed they were put in a vulnerable position in society because they were not permitted to **go forth** from their homes and families as a man might, and they were limited by what they could do to support themselves.

The sangha first created by the Buddha was exclusively for monks, not monks and nuns. Then, as now, this was the tendency with most monastic orders of all religions worldwide, following the traditional values of most societies. The presence of women in Buddhist monastic life was feared for their capacity to

> **KEYWORD**
>
> Go-forth: term used to describe those who left home and hearth to devote themselves to a spiritual quest.

arouse desires in men, and for the risk of disruption to monastic life which they posed. Any celibate society which aims to rid itself of desires, attachments and worldliness would be placed under great strain if members of both sexes lived and worked together.

Five years after the Buddha's enlightenment, and soon after the death of his father Suddhodana, the Buddha was approached by his stepmother. She asked to be ordained as a nun, and brought many other women of the Sakya tribe wanting to do likewise. Some of these women might have needed the support of the sangha because male relatives had already joined, or had died, but others were genuine seekers as a result of their life experiences. Three times the Buddha is said to have refused them, perhaps mindful of the disapproval of the powerful Brahmin priests, for whom the idea of women achieving spiritual advancement was sacrilegious, or perhaps concerned for the distraction the presence of nuns might cause to celibate monks. Ananda, the Buddha's cousin, is said to have asked on the women's behalf a further three times, finally persuading the Buddha to relent by gaining an admission that women are as capable of liberation from cravings as men. His stepmother was eventually ordained as the first Buddhist nun, but the Buddha would not accept that women would be able to achieve the status of arhant. This is surprising as we learn in the *Jataka Tales* that the Buddha had lived past lives in the form of a woman.

Ananda often championed women's causes, but he was unusual in this. He once asked the Buddha how a monk should conduct himself with women, only to be told, 'Do not see them'. When Ananda pursued his question and asked, 'But if we should see them?' The Buddha replied,

'Do not speak to them.' Ananda persisted, and asked, 'But if they should talk to us?' to which he was advised by the Buddha to, 'Keep wide awake, Ananda.'

Most Buddhist literature reveals this early ambivalence or outright antagonism to the presence of women. Buddha's final assent to the admission of women to the order was given on the understanding that nuns accept stricter rules governing their conduct than was expected of monks. In this he reflected the prevailing attitudes towards women in the wider society.

Even the Buddha's stepmother in her advanced years had to obey the Buddha's injunction that all nuns of whatever seniority should rise and salute if a monk came near, even the youngest and newest monk in the sangha. Some nuns, even given these stricter rules, still found greater freedom within the sangha than they

KEYWORD

Ordination: the formal ceremony for accepting a new monk (or nun) into an order.

would have experienced in the society outside. Separate orders of nuns were formed which solved some gender conflicts. After many years, whether from plagues or social upheavals, or lack of support from the laity, fewer and fewer nuns came forward for ordination and the older ones were dying out. It was a requirement for **ordination** that there be a certain number of members of the sangha, so when this precondition could not be met, the women's orders gradually died out.

On the death of the Buddha, local women who wanted to see his body were prevented from doing so in accordance with the non-Buddhist belief that their presence would be a defilement of the body. The peer pressure of society appears to have outweighed justice and the classless intentions of the Buddha's teaching where women were concerned.

BUDDHIST ART

During his lifetime, the Buddha discouraged personal attention in favour of the teaching so for a long time after his death he was not represented figuratively. This situation was changed by the first or second century BC by ordinary people who missed the tradition of paying respect to images. Today most schools use images of the Buddha as objects of veneration and the Buddha and his teaching still inspires many artists.

The Buddha is usually shown at the moment of some achievement, a particular moment in his life, in a specific act or state of mind (such as when meditating at the time of his enlightenment), lying on his side in repose on his deathbed, at the moment of nirvana, or when totally emaciated from fasting before he realized the middle way.

The Buddha's hand gestures, or **mudras**, in paintings and sculptures are highly significant. These gestures express a mood or action, such as compassion, meditation, setting in motion of the Wheel of the Law, or blessing the earth at the moment of his enlightenment. In addi-

KEYWORD

Mudras: particular gestures made with the hands which indicate an inner state or outward act.

tion to the Buddha's position and gestures, characteristic marks also indicate his status. These are the marks by which his great future was foretold in his infancy. The following are a few of the better known characteristics by which artists make clear who their subject is:

* elongated ear lobes are said to indicate the wearing of heavy earrings during his early princely life;
* wheel marks on the hands or the soles of the feet;
* tight curls all over the head;
* a protuberance on the crown of his head, sometimes shown as a chignon of hair;
* a mark on his forehead;
* brows shaped like a swallow's wings.

The Buddha's exploits in former lives, as told in the *Jataka Tales*, are visually interpreted in many art forms. Paintings are particularly used to remind the onlooker of aspects of the life, legends and exploits in the former births of the Buddha. These show the future Buddha acting with compassion, generosity, wisdom and in other meritorious ways. By these exploits we see how right behaviour accumulates positive karma, and in the Buddha's case are sufficient to lead to his last, illustrious life.

The **lotus flower** is a favourite symbol in some schools of Buddhism. The way it grows with its head, or flower, in the heavens while its body remains in the mud, is seen as an encouragement to human potential and aspiration. Often the Buddha is shown seated on a thousand-petalled lotus flower to suggest his attainment and perfection.

The **mandala** is a symbolic representation in the form of a circle, usually depicting the universe, its many levels and their occupants. Mandalas of symbolic patterns are much used

KEYWORDS

Lotus flower: plant used by Buddhists as a spiritual metaphor.

Mandala: a symbolic circular representation of the universe.

Pagoda: temple or sacred building (Hindu or Buddhist).

Calligraphy: the art of fine handwriting.

as the focus for meditation and mental concentration, particularly in Tibetan Buddhism. A square within a circle represents the earth. The colours used represent qualities of the Buddha for contemplation, such as white for purity, or blue for truth. Mandalas may be painted, or created from many coloured sands carefully poured onto the ground to make the intricate symbolic picture. These exquisite creations are often produced for a particular ceremony, after which the sand is swept away obliterating the image, a reminder that all created things must change and perish.

Buddhist architecture in some parts of the world also reflects beliefs about the universe to be contemplated by their visitors. Some temples are approached via a series of terraces, each symbolic of a level of existence. The architecture of stupas, temples and monasteries, the layout of formal gardens and **pagodas**, the great golden statues and fine **calligraphy** have all served to venerate and honour the memory of the effort and achievement of the man who became the Buddha, and other Buddhist saints and Arhants.

The mandala is much used as a focus for meditation.

✳ ✳ ✳ ✳ *SUMMARY* ✳ ✳ ✳ ✳

● In the absence of teaching by the Buddha about other realms, early Buddhists continued to believe in traditional Hindu cosmological explanations.

● The sangha treated nuns more strictly than monks, perhaps fearful that they might distract celibate monks.

● A mandala is a focus for meditation. It consists of a symbolic representation of the cosmos and its inhabitants. These are widely used in the later schools of Buddhism such as developed in Tibet.

● In accordance with the Buddha's wishes, early Buddhists did not depict his image. Later Buddhist artists did so from a desire to respect and be inspired by him.

12 Buddhism Today

The Buddha knew his teaching would be difficult to comprehend, let alone to live by. Many would aspire, but few if any would achieve nirvana. Few seekers would be able to sacrifice all that they know and hold dear. To rid oneself of the concept of self is like asking the captain of a ship to scuttle the vessel he believes keeps him afloat. Desires and aversions help shape who we believe we are, so consequently we relinquish them reluctantly. We prefer the false reality of our identity, and from that belief weave a web of expectations, likes, dislikes and future hopes which entrap us.

The Buddha realized that people whose lives were filled with desires would not want to hear that their own actions were determining their karma and rebirth, yet to desire enlightenment is to create another craving which will ultimately also have to be overcome. However, a life lived ethically creates peace and happiness and conditions a better rebirth, even if nirvana is not achieved, and so the Buddha decided even if only a few were willing to make the effort, his teaching would be worthwhile.

THE GLOBAL SPREAD OF BUDDHISM TODAY

Buddhism spread because it was popular, especially to members of the low castes of India whose social outlook was bleak. Buddhist teaching was in plain language and offered everyone, regardless of their social position, the chance to change their life for the better. Improvement was both spiritual and practical. Buddhism offered hope of liberation in this life, or at least an improved rebirth in the next, and a caste-free wider society.

Buddhism as a discipline or religion was founded in India around the fifth century BC and flourished globally, yet by the twelfth century AD it had almost died out in its country of origin. Though estimates suggest there are over 500 million Buddhists in the world today, it is now a minor religion in Asia, where it is practiced mainly in the south.

Buddhism has proved to be especially popular in the western world.

The spread of Buddhism to more distant countries was more lasting and came about as a result of missionary monks and lay people who travelled for political or economic reasons, each taking with them their beliefs and religious practices. These travellers would set up new communities wherever they settled. Buddhist practices were adapted somewhat to fit in with local traditions and politics (women are again ordained as nuns in the west) and in the process different schools developed, but the essential elements of the Buddha's teaching remain the same whatever the school, and wherever Buddhism is practiced.

POSTSCRIPT

The concept of personal attainment offered in Buddhist teaching has suited the individualism of the modern age which may account for its increasing popularity. This is not without irony. Although the life and discoveries of Siddhartha Gautama, the Buddha, undoubtedly inspired millions, he acted purely from a sense of compassion with no wish for personal recognition. His teaching was intended to share the means to escape suffering; no more, no less.

Right beliefs, Right knowledge, Right conduct

✳ ✳ ✳ ✳ SUMMARY ✳ ✳ ✳ ✳

- There are over 500 million practicing Buddhists in the world today.

- Buddhism waned in India after the introduction of Christianity and Islam, but is steadily becoming popular again.

- The teachings of the Buddha are particularly suited to the modern ideal of personal effort and achievement.

GLOSSARY

Anitya The impermanence of all that we experience.

Bodhi Enlightenment.

Bodhisattva A Buddha-to-be before attaining enlightenment.

Dependent origination Buddhist explanation of a causal universe; cause and effect.

Dhyana Meditative state of concentration.

Four Noble Truths The essential expounded by the Buddha in his first sermon.

Karman Ancient Aryan word for the act of sacrifice.

Middle Way The moderate Buddhist way, neither self-indulgent nor austere.

Nirvana (Nibbana) The realization of no-self and freedom from cravings and attachment.

Pali The commonly spoken language of South Asia when the oral history and teachings of Buddhism was written down. It could be written in any script-form.

Samadhi A deep state of meditation and altered awareness.

Samsara The belief in perpetual rebirth according to unexhausted karma. Nirvana, as achieved by the Buddha, brings liberation from future rebirth and more sorrow.

Sanskrit The language of the priestly caste at the time of Buddha, and of the ancient Hindu and Aryan religious texts. Not the language of ordinary people.

Ten Ethical Precepts (Sometimes only the five are listed.) Abstain from killing stealing, improper sexual conduct, lying or improper speech, using intoxicants, eating other than at prescribed times, singing and dancing, using cosmetics, sleeping on a comfortable bed, accepting gold and silver.

Wheel of the Law It is often depicted as an eight-spoked wheel to represent the Eightfold Path to liberation from ignorance.

Wheel of Becoming A way to describe the endless births and rebirths until, in enlightenment, we become free from the effects of karma.

FURTHER READING

The Buddhist Handbook. A Complete Guide to Buddhist Teaching and Practice, John Snelling, Rider: Random House UK Ltd, London, 1992.

Buddhist Scriptures. Selected and translated by Edward Conze, Penguin Books, 1959.

Digha-Nikaya T.W. Rhys Davids and J.E. Carpenter (eds.), 3 volumes, London, 1890–1911.

The Dhammapada, Translated from the Pali by Juan Mascaro, Penguin Books, 1973.

The Foundations of Buddhism, Rupert Gethin, Oxford University Press, 1998.

The Social Dimensions of Early Buddhism, Dr Uma Chakravarti, Oxford University Press, 1987.

The Wisdom of the Buddha, Jean Boisselier, Thames and Hudson: New Horizons, London, 1994.

The World of Buddhism, Heinz Bechert and Richard Gombrich (eds.), Thames & Hudson, London, 1991.

The World's Religions, Ninian Smart (ed.), 2nd edition, Cambridge University Press, 1998.

INDEX